CULINARY HERBS
AND CONDIMENTS

Culinary Herbs
and Condiments

BY

M. GRIEVE, F.R.H.S.

DOVER PUBLICATIONS, INC.

NEW YORK

This Dover edition, first published in 1971, is an unabridged republication of the work originally published by Harcourt, Brace and Company, Inc. in 1934.

International Standard Book Number: 0-486-21513-X
Library of Congress Catalog Card Number: 70-153058

Manufactured in the United States of America
Dover Publications, Inc.
180 Varick Street
New York, N. Y. 10014

PREFACE TO THE AMERICAN EDITION

WHEN the pilgrim Fathers set sail in the *Mayflower* to found a home in a new land, they left a country where the virtues of herbs were highly appreciated and their cultivation assiduously practised. No house of importance lacked a herb garden, or a still-room where numerous useful and delightful confections were made from the garden's fragrant produce.

With the passing of time, both still-rooms and herb gardens began to disappear. Certain herbs, it is true, were grown on a commercial scale; but, by the time of the outbreak of the European War, the industry had dwindled to small dimensions; and Great Britain was faced with an unpleasant realisation that she had become very largely dependent on Teutonic sources for her main supply of medicinal and other herbs. An increased interest in herb cultivation was the natural result. This increased interest has been given a fresh lease of life as a result of Great Britain's new fiscal policy; and it has also manifested itself in no uncertain manner in America.

The result has been the publication of a number of interesting and useful books on the subject, some of which, however, suffer from the disadvantage of being mainly compilations from older works.

There is, I think, room for a short, practical manual; and, in this book, I have endeavoured to fill the gap. Having been engaged in herb-growing for many years, I am able to write from practical experience, the fruits of which I offer readers.

It is becoming more and more clearly realised that a well-cooked meal is not merely one that is wholesome and nutritious. In addition, it must be palatable. The importance of flavour can hardly be overestimated; and for flavouring food, few things are more useful than fresh herbs culled from one's own garden.

In this book I have endeavoured to tell the amateur gardener and the housewife all they need to know about this class of herb. Although originally addressed to readers in my own country, I think there is little in it that will not be found to appeal just as readily to the American housewife or amateur gardener. I have endeavoured carefully to describe the chief culinary herbs grown in Great Britain, giving details concerning their cultivation and their uses in the kitchen. The same herbs can be grown equally well in North America, the same methods of cultivation and employment being applicable.

There is a special section containing recipes for home-made wines, herbal beers and other herbal beverages; and I think American readers will be interested in these recipes of olden days, in which herbs are either the chief ingredients or add to the confections a certain indefinable charm.

There are also special sections dealing with condiments, culinary oils, etc., and with the choice and cleansing of culinary utensils, which, it is hoped, will prove of practical interest and value.

M. G.

CONTENTS

CONTENTS

PART I

SWEET OR CULINARY HERBS—THEIR CULTIVATION AND PROPAGATION— PLANT LIST

PART I

SWEET OR CULINARY HERBS

SWEET or Culinary Herbs may be defined as plants whose green parts, ripe seeds or tender roots have an aromatic flavour and fragrance due to a volatile oil, or to some other chemical substance peculiar to the individual species. Owing to the fragrance most of these herbs possess, they have been called SWEET, and from their use in cookery for the purpose of imparting their characteristic flavour to soups, stews, dressings, sauces and salads, they are popularly called "culinary," though this term is less appropriate than the former, since many other herbs such as cabbage, spinach, kale, etc., are also, strictly speaking, culinary herbs; but these, being used as vegetables and not for flavouring, are more accurately known as POTHERBS, and others, also employed for the table, but in an uncooked state, we distinguish as SALAD HERBS.

ORIGIN OF SWEET HERBS

Most of the sweet herbs in question, though now found growing freely in every well-stocked kitchen garden in this country, were originally natives of the Mediterranean region, and were in use by the nations bordering its shores from the earliest days, long before our era. There are references in both the Old and New Testament to various herbs—Mint, Dill, Rue, Cumin and others—and among the Greeks and

3

Romans, many of our garden herbs were held in great esteem, and employed by them and through the Middle Ages, probably far more than at the present time.

Of the thirty odd plants that from their uses may be designated culinary herbs, it is to be noted that the majority belong to one or other of the two great plant families, Labiatæ—the Deadnettle family—and Umbelliferæ—the Hemlock family. To the former, the Sage, Thyme and Mints belong; to the latter, the Parsley, Fennel and Dill. With the exception of Tarragon and Tansy, which belong to the Compositæ, or Dandelion family, and Parsley and its relations, all the more important herbs used for the sake of their leaves belong to the Labiatæ, while all the herbs whose seeds are used for flavouring belong to the Umbelliferæ.

The Herbs belonging to the Labiatæ whose culinary uses in the present or past are sufficiently important for our consideration are:—

Balm (Melissa officinalis),
Basil (Ocimum Basilicum and O. minimum),
Catmint (Nepeta Cataria),
Clary Sage (Salvia Sclarea),
Horehound (Marrubium vulgare),
Hyssop (Hyssopus Officinalis),
Marjoram (Origanum Onites, O. Marjorana and O. vulgare),
Rosemary (Rosmarinus officinalis),
Sage (Salvia officinalis),

Savory, Summer (Satureia hortensis),
    „   Winter   („   montana),
Spearmint (Mentha spicata),
Thyme (Thymus vulgaris).

All these plants are characterised by having square stems, opposite, simple leaves and two-lipped flowers, which are placed in the axils of the leaves, sometimes singly, but generally several together, forming little rings or whorls, the various tiers of which often constitute loose or compact spikes. On fertilisation—mainly by bees—four little seedlike fruits or nutlets are produced, protected by the calyx, which remains attached to the plant. The leaves are mostly sprinkled over with tiny glands, containing a volatile oil, upon which the fragrance and piquancy of the individual species depend.

The most important sweet herbs belonging to the order Umbelliferæ are—in order of importance—

Parsley (Carum Petroselinum),
Dill (Anethum graveolens),
Fennel Fœniculum vulgare and var. dulce),
Angelica (Archangelica officinalis),
Anise (Pimpinella Anisum),
Caraway (Carum Carvi),
Coriander (Coriandrum sativum),
Chervil (Anthriscus Cerefolium),
Cumin (Cuminum Cyminum),
Lovage (Levisticum officinale).

The stems of umbelliferous plants are cylindrical and usually hollow; the leaves placed alternately on the stem are generally compound (*i.e.,* cut into right up to the mid-rib, not merely toothed, as in Labiatæ), and the base of each stalk broadens out into a sheath which clasps the stem. The flowers are small, generally white or pinkish, sometimes yellow, and mostly arranged in umbels, *i.e.,* the stalks of each little group spring all from one point, like the ribs of an umbrella, these umbels, or umbellules, being generally also grouped each on separate stalks converging to a central point—thus forming a compound umbel, which terminates the main stem. The fruits are composed of two seedlike, dry portions, or carpels, each containing a single seed and usually separating when ripe. Each carpel, or half of the fruit, bears five longitudinal, prominent ribs, and several lesser ones. In the spaces between the ribs are numerous oil ducts or vittæ, to which the aromatic properties of the fruits are due. Though the oil is generally also found in other parts of the plant, it is present to the greatest extent in the fruits.

With the exception of Tarragon, the sweet herbs belonging to the great order COMPOSITÆ are less important. The distinguishing feature of this family of plants is that the flowers are arranged in tightly-packed heads on a disc, or "capitulum," which is surrounded by closely fitting, leaf-like bracts, termed the "involucre," forming a kind of cup. Only four plants belonging to this family are deserving of our consideration as sweet herbs, though others, such as Dandelion and Chicory, are also useful in the kitchen as salad plants. These four are:—

Marigold (Calendula officinalis),
Southernwood (Artemisia Abrotanum),
Tansy (Tanacetum vulgare),
Tarragon (Artemisia Dracunculus).

To the representatives of these three great families may be added:—

Rue (Ruta graveolens) belonging to the order Rutaceæ,
Borage (Borago officinalis)   „   Boraginaceæ,
Burnet (Poterium Sanguisorba)   „   Rosaceæ,
Sweet Bay (Laurus nobilis)   „   Lauraceæ

Mint, Parsley, Sage, Thyme and Marjoram may be considered the principal sweet herbs now in general use, but the many others enumerated, which formerly were made use of to a greater degree than now, might well with advantage to our cuisine be more widely known, and deserve more attention than is generally given them.

GENERAL SURVEY OF THE USES OF THE VARIOUS HERBS

The greatest demand nowadays is undoubtedly for Parsley, on account of its being used more extensively as a garnish than any other herb. As a flavouring agent, it has probably a wider application than any of the other herbs. It is chiefly employed in dressings with mild meats, such as chicken, turkey, veal, and with fish, also for soups, stews and sauces, especially those used with boiled meats, fricassees and fish.

SAGE, being a strongly flavoured plant, is used chiefly with such fat meats as pork, goose, duck and some kinds of game. It is used to flavour sausage meat, and in some countries with certain kinds of cheese. In the United States it is more widely used than any other culinary herb.

THYME and SAVORY are used about equally, chiefly like Parsley, both, in addition (especially Thyme), being used in certain kinds of sausage.

MARJORAM is similarly employed, though to a lesser degree, and next in favour come BALM, BASIL and FENNEL. All these milder herbs are often mixed, the blend resulting in a new

7

compound flavour, the mixture being utilised in the same manner as the individual herbs.

TARRAGON and SPEARMINT are used in a different manner from those just mentioned, Tarragon chiefly as a decoction, in the flavouring of fish sauces, or in the preparation of vinegar; and MINT, with vinegar, in the dressing with lamb, or as a flavouring to green peas or pea soup.

DILL is probably the most important of the herbs whose seeds, rather than their leaves, are used in flavouring food other than confectionery, being employed greatly in the flavouring of cucumber pickle, largely consumed on the Continent, and to a more limited degree by foreign residents in this country.

GARNISH HERBS

Though Parsley is more widely used than any other herb as a garnish, several others, FENNEL, TANSY, SAVORY, THYME, MARJORAM, BASIL and BALM make pretty garnishes, but are rarely used (except Fennel, for fish) though their pleasing effect may be heightened by adding here and there a few herb flowers, such as Thyme or Savory.

HERBS AS DECORATION IN THE HOUSE AND GARDEN

Sweet Herbs can also be used decoratively in the house and garden, as well as in the kitchen. A charming bouquet may be arranged of the delicate flowers of Marjoram, the pale pink blossoms of Thyme and the bright yellow umbels of Fennel, mixed with fragrant sprigs of lemon Balm and the bluish, finely-cut leaves of Rue—a bouquet dainty in appearance and in sweetness hard to excel. And not only is such a dainty bunch of herb flowers decorative, but its pleasant aromatic odour, from its antiseptic properties, is of value for the general health of the house, and especially for the sick room, where the scent of these aromatic herbs has a refreshing and invigorating influence on the atmosphere, being not so cloying as the perfume of most flowers, and helping to keep drinks in a room sweet. The presence of these herbs will also greatly tend to keep a sick room free of troublesome insects, who have a distaste for the scent of nearly all of them. Many of the herbs in a dried state, such as Rosemary, Rue, and to a still greater extent Lavender, have, moreover, from olden times been employed as deodorisers, the odours given off by them when burnt being both healthy and pleasant.

In the garden, a most decorative border can also be arranged with herbs—edging and rockery can be USEFUL as well as pleasing to the eye. For instance, Sages backed by late flowering Orange Lilies go very well together, and being in flower at the same time, make an effective grouping. Again, the calyces of Sage flowers remain on the plants well into late summer and give a lovely haze of reddish spikes; the smell of these seeding spikes is very distinct from the smell of the leaves, and much more like that of lemon-scented Verbena, pungent, aromatic and most refreshing. Catmint and Hyssop grown together make a charming border, the soft blues of the blossoms blending pleasingly, and the grouping being still more effective if Lavender and Rosemary are grown behind them, especially if the bed be backed by a grey stone wall.

HOW TO PREPARE A HERB DINNER

We have touched on the uses of the various herbs with regard to meat dishes, but it is easy to serve a tasty little luncheon for vegetarians, in which each course owes its distinguishing feature to the common culinary herbs, though before going into the matter, a "Dinner of Herbs" may not sound very attractive.

A PARSLEY SOUP may start the meal, and may be prepared from the following recipe, much used in Belgium: thicken flour and butter together as for melted butter sauce, and when properly cooked thin to soup consistency with milk. Season with salt, pepper and onion juice. Boil up, and just before serving add sufficient finely-chopped parsley to colour the soup green. Serve with fried croutons.

A SAVOURY OMELETTE may follow the soup. Prepare the omelette in the ordinary manner, and before folding it add a layer of chopped Thyme, Tarragon and Chives; or the herbs may be stirred into the beaten-up eggs before cooking the omelette.

Instead of an omelette, savoury eggs stuffed with sweet herbs and served in cream may be preferred. Boil the eggs hard, cut them lengthwise and remove the yolks. Mash and season them, adding the herbs, as finely chopped as possible. Shape again like yolks and replace in the whites. Cover with a hot cream sauce or melted butter sauce and serve at once.

Both Savoury Omelette and Stuffed Eggs may be garnished with shredded parsley.

With the eggs may be served a dish of Onion Potatoes, prepared by placing in alternate layers slices of the two vegetables, with little lumps of butter, seasoning with pepper and salt, adding milk even with the top layer, and baking till done.

A MIXED SALAD may follow: to the heart leaves of Lettuces add Nasturtium leaves and blossoms, Tarragon, Chives, Mint, Thyme and any other green leaves of aromatic herbs. Dress with a simple oil and vinegar dressing, omitting sugar, mustard or other flavouring, as the leaves themselves are piquant enough.

With this Salad, Sandwiches may be passed round, made with lettuce or nasturtium dressed with mayonnaise. The mayonnaise dressing may be made more piquant by the addition of chopped Chives, or Tarragon, or Thyme. Such Herb Sandwiches in different varieties will be found an appetising addition also to the picnic hamper: Sweet Fennel and the tender leaves of Sage, Marjoram and other herbs finely chopped, mixed with cream cheese, make a piquant layer between two thin slices of bread.

The luncheon may be concluded with a cream cheese into which, with a silver knife, has been worked any of these herbs (or any two of them that agree with it well), served with toasted biscuits; or the biscuits may be toasted with ordinary cheese, over which sage and thyme are grated.

SUMMER DRINKS

Some of the sweet herbs may be used to give additional flavour to summer drinks: Spearmint (the ordinary garden mint) adds a pleasing pungency to lemonade, and the blue flowers of Borage have long been employed in like manner, and are often also added to a mixture of honey and water, to grape juice, or to raspberry vinegar and other fruit drinks.

CANDIED ROOTS

The aromatic roots of Lovage may be candied, and form a pleasant substitute for the preserved ginger imported from the East.

CULTIVATION AND PROPAGATION OF
CULINARY HERBS

It is a popular error to say "ordinary kitchen herbs will grow anywhere," for to produce medicinal plants, among which those also used for culinary purposes must be included, it is necessary to garden thoughtfully, *i.e.,* to know and practise, not only all the essentials of good gardening, but in addition, *science* is required, to get the highest medicinal qualities in the plant, for a plant may be well grown and "look nice" and yet be grown under such conditions that the chemical constituents needed may not be present in sufficient degree. To produce herbs successfully needs a higher form of gardening than the ordinarily accepted good work, for special scientific knowledge must be added to the everyday gardener's practical rules.

In choosing the SITUATION of the Herb Garden, it is in general advisable to choose a south aspect and a smooth, gentle slope, but whatever the nature of the surface available and the aspect, the herbs should always be given the most sunny spots in the garden, free from the shade of trees, fences or buildings, as the development of the volatile oils on which the value of the herb depends is greater when the plants are grown in full sunshine.

As to SOIL, a light, sandy loam, with a porous subsoil, ensuring good drainage, will be the most favourable, as it is warmed quickly and is easily worked. A CLAY LOAM is less desirable, as it cannot be worked so early in the season or after a spell of rain, and a very sandy soil is too porous and apt to scorch the plants. Good cultivation will, however, do much to remedy original defects in the soil.

For obtaining the best results in aromatic herbs a very

rich soil is not required, as in such soils the growth is apt to be too rank, the quantity of volatile oil being small in proportion to the leafage produced.

Preparation of the Soil should commence in the first days of spring, well-decayed manure being spread at the rate of a bushel or more to the square yard, and dug in with the garden fork as soon as the soil is dry enough to crumble readily, the ground being turned over thoroughly until a fine tilth is obtained. On heavy land, the soil should be dug over in the autumn and left rough for the frost to act on the lumps, which will crumble when raked or harrowed in the spring.

A fine tilth having been obtained, the seeds may be sown or plants transplanted into the bed. For the rest of the season the surface must be kept loose and open by stirring every week or ten days and after every shower, not only to keep weeds in check, but to keep the surface layer in a state of powder, which acts as a mulch, preventing loss of moisture from the lower layers around the roots.

Propagation. Most herbs can readily be propagated by means of Seeds. Some, however, such as Tarragon, which does not produce seed in this country, and several other perennial kinds, are propagated by division, layers or cuttings. As the seeds in many instances are very small and slow to germinate, they are often sown in shallow boxes or seed pans, and when large enough to be handled transplanted to somewhat deeper boxes—a couple of inches being allowed between the plants, being finally transplanted into permanent quarters in the garden when conditions are favourable, the soil moist and warm, and the season settled. The seed may also be sown out-of-doors in drills, about the end of April or early May, and thinned out as it comes up, but the process just described is more economical. Fennel, Basil, Knotted

Marjoram and Dill are generally sown out-of-doors, as they are not subject to the attacks of birds, as many other seeds are.

LAYERING. Many of the perennial herbs, such as Sage, Thyme and Savory are easily propagated by layering, the stems being pegged down and covered lightly with earth. These plants are "stem-rooted" and, under favourable conditions of moisture and temperature, roots are generally formed in three or four weeks, wherever the stem is in contact with the earth, when the stem may be separated from the parent plant and removed to new quarters. If there are several branches on a stem, each of these may be used as a new little plant, provided it has some roots, or has a rooted portion of the main stem attached to it.

Layering is the simplest and most satisfactory method of propagation under ordinary conditions, for the stems are practically certain to take root if left undisturbed, and the rooted plants, if transplanted with ordinary care, will rarely fail to grow. Thus less time is taken than with plants grown from cuttings, and much less than with those raised from seed. In short, stock raised by layering will produce a crop sooner than the plants obtained by other modes of propagation undertaken at the same time.

CUTTINGS. Those herbs like the Mints and those related to them, which have creeping underground stems, are easily propagated by means of cuttings—each joint of the stem producing a new plant if placed in rather moist soil.

The other perennial and biennial herbs are readily propagated by means of stem cuttings or "slips." The cuttings are made either of fully-ripened wood of the preceding or the current season, or they may be of firm—not succulent—green stems. The cuttings should be about 4 or 5 inches long. After trimming off all but a few of the upper leaves, the cuttings should be plunged nearly full depth in light, porous, well-drained loam, and left undisturbed and well shaded till they show signs of growth, when they may be transplanted. They must never be allowed to become dry, and green wood cuttings made during the summer should, especially, always be given the coolest, shadiest corner in the garden. Cuttings taken in spring may be set out in permanent quarters as soon as rooted, but summer cuttings should generally be left in their beds until the following spring, though they may be removed for winter use to the greenhouse.

DIVISION. Sometimes clumps of herbs of spreading growth, such as Mint, are divided into pieces about 6 inches square, a sharp spade being employed, and the squares placed in new quarters and firmly pressed into the soil. If division is done in early spring, before growth starts, little damage is done to the plants. It is not too late, even early in May, to increase the stock of Mint, Balm, Marjoram, Thyme, Hyssop and Savory, by off-sets or division of the roots. If done in showery weather they start away freely, and make good plants before late summer. They must be well watered.

The artificial methods of propagation, especially by cuttings or layers, have the advantage of propagation by means of seeds, in the certainty of perpetuating the desired characters of any individual plant that may prove to have specially good points. Such plants, if more productive than the others among which they have appeared, should always be utilised as stock, as the yield of the plantation will thereby be increased.

By expending a little more time, any desired number of plants may, of course, be obtained from seed.

TRANSPLANTING. The ordinary methods of transplanting apply equally to herbs. It may not often be practicable to grow the plants in small flower-pots and set them in the garden when they have formed a small ball of roots, though this is the ideal way. A more generally followed and successful proceeding is to grow them in the greenhouse, in seed pans and then in shallow boxes, set several inches apart, as soon as large enough to handle, and where they should be allowed to grow for several weeks and form a mass of roots. When to be set in the garden in permanent quarters, the plants should be broken carefully apart by hand with as little loss of root as possible. If grown in little nursery beds in the open, or in hot beds or cold frames, the plants should be "pricked out," *i.e.,* transplanted when very small, to a second nursery bed, in order to make them strong and sturdy before being removed to their final quarters.

Transplanting should only take place when the ground is moist, as it is immediately after being dug. An ideal time for transplanting is just before a fall of rain, though immediately after one is almost as good. It is better to transplant in cloudy weather and towards evening, than in sunny weather and in the morning.

The plants should always be taken up with as little loss of roots as possible, be kept exposed to the air as short a time as possible, and when placed again in the ground should have the soil packed in very firmly about their roots. After setting, the surface soil should be loosened, to act as a mulch and prevent excessive loss of moisture from the lower layers round the roots.

HARVESTING AND PREPARATION FOR USE. We may divide Herbs into three groups: those whose LEAVES yield the aromatic flavour, such as Parsley, Mint, Sage, Thyme, etc., those whose SEED is used, such as Dill, Anise, Caraway and Fennel, and those whose ROOTS or STEMS are employed, such as Lovage and Angelica.

Foliage herbs are employed either green or dried, as a

decoction or infusion.

When used green, if newly gathered, the herbs yield their aromatic properties to the fullest extent, and add a finer and more delicate flavour to sauces and stews than when used in a dry condition. Again, in salads, they should always be used green, as specks of dried herbs would spoil the look of a salad, and both these and a decoction of the herbs would impart a greatly inferior flavour to the salad as compared with the crisp, fresh leaves.

As most herbs, however, cannot be obtained throughout the year, they are dried or infused for use when the green leaves will no longer grow in the open.

Every household in the kingdom keeps for winter use a bottle or tin of powdered sweet herbs for flavouring soups, entrées and vegetables, and it seems almost incredible that before the war we annually imported many thousand pounds' worth of dried and powdered ordinary culinary herbs, such as Sage, Thyme, Mint, Parsley, etc., to meet this demand. This should have been quite unnecessary, as they can so easily be grown here, with a minimum of trouble and outlay. There is no reason why everyone who has a garden should not propagate and dry these herbs wherever the soil suits them, quite apart from those who may grow them on a commercial footing, to meet all home requirements and obviate the necessity of their being imported from foreign countries.

By co-operative action, these herbs might be much better grown in this country, and would probably find a large market also in the United States and in the Colonies, as they could be grown purer and freer from admixture with other species, than is the case with those imported yearly by the shipload from south European countries, where, as in Spain, numerous varieties of Thyme occur in the wild condition.

HARVESTING OF THE HERBS. For whatever purpose and in whatever condition they are to be used, the aromatic flavours of foliage herbs are always best in well-developed leaves and shoots of plants in full growth, and the flavours are strongest and most characteristic just before the flowers break into blossom. These aromatic properties are due to essential oils, which are dissipated by heat; they are also present to a greater extent in the morning than after the sun has reached its full height. To obtain the full fragrance of sweet herbs, therefore, especially for drying, they should be harvested just when coming into flower and be gathered only on a fine day, in the morning, as soon as the dew is off, before the hot sun has taken any oil from the leaves. All leaves that are withered, stained or insect-eaten, or otherwise not in perfect condition should be removed. All herbs with at all woody stems should then be tied loosely in bunches and hung to dry on stems in the open, if the day be warm, though in half shade, and preferably under cover, to avoid damping in case of showers. When dried in strong light out-of-doors, it is advisable to cover the bunches with thin paper, to prevent the colour being injured by the light. The herbs must be brought indoors to a dry room or shed at night, before there is any chance of becoming damp from dew. When the leaves are quite dry and crisp, artificial heat near a stove may be used to dry the stems after the leaves are quite shrivelled, to finish the operation. Short-stemmed species and leaves may be dried on wire trays or wooden racks, placed a few feet above the ground to ensure their being exposed to a current of air, being placed in a single layer so that the warm air circulates to all parts to be dried.

Drying may also be carried out indoors, in a hot, sunny attic, the window being left open at the top by day, so that there is a current of air and the room does not become steamy. The door may also be left open. The herbs can either be hung, bunched, over strings, or if the stems are succulent, they can be placed on canvas or wire-mesh trays, or placed on butter-cloth, stented, *i.e.,* if hooks are placed beneath the window and on the opposite wall, the butter-cloth can be attached by rings sewn on each side of it and hooked on, so that it is stretched quite taut. Failing sun, any ordinary shed, fitted with racks and shelves, can be used for drying herbs, provided it is ventilated near the roof and has a warm current of air, caused by an ordinary coke or anthracite stove. Empty glasshouses can be readily adapted in drying sheds, especially if heated by pipes and the glass shaded; ventilation is essential and there must be no tank in the house to cause steaming; the roof also must be quite watertight.

Two or three days will be sufficient for thorough drying, which is essential; this should be carried out in a gentle heat never above 100° Fahr. and quickly, that the aromatic odour may be preserved—the quicker herbs are dried, the better, as "heating" or fermentation may thereby be prevented. The best drying temperature for drying aromatic herbs is about 70° F. Their strength and fineness of flavour depend greatly on their harvesting and drying.

Oven drying of herbs should be avoided, as the oil is apt to evaporate somewhat before the leaves get dry. The bunches should be nearly equal in length and uniform in size to facilitate packing and placed when dry in air-tight boxes or tins to prevent re-absorption of moisture. The leaves may also be stripped from the stems as soon as thoroughly dry and rubbed through a fine sieve so as to be freed from stalks as much as possible, or pounded into a mortar and thus powdered, stored in stoppered bottles, or tins rendered air-tight.

If prepared for market and not for home use, the rubbed herbs will, of course, command a higher price than the bunched herbs, and should be put up in tins or bottles containing a quantity of uniform weight. If there be the slightest trace of moisture in the powder, it should, before bottling, be dried to ensure against mould.

Powdered herbs should never be stored in paper or pasteboard packages, since the delicate oils readily diffuse through the paper, and in course of time the powder becomes valueless for flavouring purposes. This loss of flavour is particularly noticeable with Sage, which even when kept in tins or air-tight bottles, only keeps its flavour for two years. The practice, therefore, of hanging up herbs in loose bundles in a storeroom and leaving them till required, whether covered with paper to preserve them from dust or not, is not to be recommended, as they soon lose their fragrance. Sometimes, however, when the bunched herbs are dry, they are pressed into cakes and then wrapped in paper, and thus stored in air-tight boxes they will retain their flavour two or three years.

Mostly all herbs should be cut and dried before the middle or end of September, not so much for the sake of the herbs to be dried, as for the roots left in the ground. There are many kinds of herbs which tend to perish during winter if they are not cut in time to allow the plants to make short growth before the growing season comes to an end.

Except as garnishes, herbs are probably more frequently used in a dry state than in other ways. Not only can large quantities be kept in small space, but the method of drying is simpler than that of infusion or decoction, and dried herbs can be used for most purposes—stuffings, soups, stews and sauces, where their fine particles are not objected to. In the case of clear soups dried herbs can still be used, the particles being removed, before serving, by straining.

To make good infusions, the freshly-gathered foliage—which must be quite clean—is packed into stoppered jars, covered with the choicest vinegar, and the jars kept tightly closed for a couple of weeks, when the fluid is strained off into another jar and is ready for use, though care must be taken to ascertain its strength and the quantity to use. In the case of Mint, the leaves are very finely chopped before being bottled, and both liquid and leaves are employed.

An objection to such decoctions is that the flavour of vinegar is not always desired in a culinary preparation, as well as that of the herb itself. Tarragon, Mint and the seed herbs such as Dill are more often used in ordinary cookery as infusions than otherwise.

SEED HERBS. The time of harvesting the herbs whose seed is used, such as Dill, Anise, Caraway, etc., differs from that customary with the foliage herbs mainly in the ripeness of the plants, which are gathered as soon as the seeds show signs of maturity, but before they are ready to drop. Special care must be paid to the details of cleaning. The seed-heads, to present a good appearance, should be gathered before they become at all weather-beaten. Next, the seed must be perfectly clean, free from chaff, bits of broken stem and other debris; much depends upon the method of handling as well as upon harvesting. In threshing, care must be taken to avoid bruising the seeds, especially the oily ones, by pounding too hard, or by trampling upon them. Threshing should never be done in damp weather—always when the air is very dry.

In clear weather, after the sun has dried off the dew, the ripe plants or seed-heads are harvested and spread thinly on stout, closely-woven cloth-ticking or sail-cloth in a warm open shed, where the air circulates freely. Generally in a few days, the tops will have become dry enough to be beaten out with a light flail or rod, care being taken not to injure the seed. It is a good plan to carry out the threshing on a sheet spread on a lawn, whereby the force of the blows will be lessened and bruising of the seeds prevented. A convenient size for the sheet is 10 feet by 10. After threshing, the seeds should be sieved to remove portions of the stalks, and then allowed to remain for several days longer in a very thin layer, being turned every day to remove the last vestige of moisture. It is also a good plan to have the drying sheet suspended a few feet from the ground, so that the air may circulate below as well as above the seed. Not less than a week for the smallest seeds, and double that time for the larger ones, is necessary to carry out drying effectively. Small quantities of seeds may be rubbed out from the heads between the palms of the hands, instead of threshing. It is imperative that the seed be dry before being put into storage packages or tins.

If infusions are to be made of the seed, the drying is, of course, unnecessary, the seed being put into the vinegar as soon as the broken bits of stem are removed by sieving, after threshing has been carried out.

HERBAL RECIPES. Old-time English Cooks made far more use of the garden products than do the modern ones. At the present day, also, Italian and Flemish cookery is prolific of recipes in which many garden herbs appear, for instance, Rosemary and Southernwood, now no longer used by us in the kitchen. Our ancestors, however, recognised the full value of our herbs, and many old recipes still exist in which they play a part.

In Warner's *Antiquities of the Culinary Art,* published in 1790, we find the following:—

"*Fritors of Erbes* (herbs). Take good erbes. Grynde hem and medle (mix) hem with floer and water; and a little zest (yeast) and salt, and frye hem in oyle and ete hem with clere hony."

"A handful of sliced horseradish root, with a handsome little faggot of Rosemary, Thyme and Winter Savory" is recommended in Cotton's sequel to *The Compleat Angler,* in the directions for dressing a trout.

In another more recent cookery book we find a recipe for Herb Powder:—

"Take fresh Marjoram, Basil, Bay-leaf, Thyme, Parsley, and dry in the sun until crisp. Pick carefully off the stalk and rub into fine powder. Add a small quantity of dried and pounded lemon peel, allowing to each ounce of herbs in powder one small saltspoon of salt and half this quantity of ground white pepper. Sift through a piece of coarse muslin, and store for use in small bottles."

This makes an excellent herb powder for flavouring purposes.

A Herb Mixture of equal proportions of Knotted Marjoram and Winter Savory, with half the quantity of Basil, Thyme and Tarragon, all rubbed to powder and kept in a closely corked bottle, is also recommended for use in forcemeat and for flavouring.

———

Having discussed sweet herbs in general, their cultivation and propagation, how to harvest them and prepare them either for market or for home consumption, it now remains to deal with each herb separately.

PLANT LIST

ANGELICA

(N.O. Umbelliferæ)

Archangelica (Officinalis Hoffm.)
Local names: Garden Angelica.
Angelica sylvestris Linn.
Local name: Wild Angelica.

USES

Candied Stems in confectionery, as a sweetmeat for flavouring jams and rhubarb.
Fruits for flavouring liqueurs and wines, and in hop bitters; also used in perfumery.
Stems, Leaf-ribs, and Roots as vegetables.
Leaves as tea, and boiled with fish.
Root as bread.
Angelica is also used medicinally.

Angelica is among those medicinal plants which grow wild, yet are only of market value when cultivated. The large variety was grown abundantly near London in moist fields for the use of its candied stems by confectioners. It is largely cultivated for medicinal purposes in Thuringia, and the roots are also imported from Spain. It is believed to be a native of Syria, whence it has spread to many cool European climates, especially Lapland and the Alps, where it has become naturalised. There are many species, but Garden Angelica is the only one of importance. The virtues of the herb are quaintly phrased by old writers, and the name itself, as well as the folk lore of all North European countries and nations, testify to the great antiquity of a belief in its merits as a protection against contagion, for purifying the blood, and for curing almost every conceivable malady. In Courland, Livonia and the Low lake lands of Pomerania and East Prussia, wild growing Angelica abounds; there, in early summer-time it is the custom of some peasants to march into the towns carrying the Angelica flower stems to offer them for sale, chanting some ancient ditty in Lettish words, so antiquated as to be unintelligible to the singers themselves. The chanted words and the tune are learnt in childhood, and may be attributed to a survival of some pagan festival. Later, the plant became linked in the popular mind with some Archangelic patronage, and associated with the spring-time festival of the Annunciation.

Dr. W. T. Fernie, in his *Meals Medicinal,* says:

"The herb known as Masterwort, or more popularly, 'Jack-jump-about,' also as Lingwort. It is grown abundantly near London, and may be cultivated in our gardens. Its peculiar resin, 'angelicin' is stimulating to the lungs. . . . Some writers have said this plant—the Archangelica—was revealed in a dream by an angel to cure the plague; others aver that it blooms on the day dedicated to Michael the Archangel (May 8th, old style), and is therefore a preservative against evil spirits and witchcraft. Angelica taken somewhat freely as a sweetmeat will cause a distaste for alcoholic liquors."

He also says:

"The Chartreuse of apples began with apple jam (called in mistake marmalade by French and German cooks); then Angelica entered as an ornamenting incrustation over the yellow, red, and white apples cemented together by the jam, the whole being boiled in a water-bath, and turned out on a plate. Here ended the apple Chartreuse, the apples assuming therein their ancient rights, and shapes. But the Angelica wandered to the brandy bottle, and Chartreuse developed into a spirit, the Carthusians becoming at length manufacturers of liqueurs."

DESCRIPTION. Angelica is a member of the natural order *Umbelliferæ*. It may be termed a perennial herbaceous plant. It is biennial only in the botanical sense of the term, that is to say, it is neither annual nor naturally perennial; the seedlings make but little advance towards maturity within 12 months, whilst old plants die off after seeding once, which event may be at a much more remote period than in the second year of growth. Only very advanced seedlings flower in their second year, and the third year of growth commonly completes the full period of life. There is another species, *Angelica heterocarpa,* which is credited with being truly perennial: it flowers a few weeks later than the biennial species and is not so ornamental in its foliage.

The roots of the Garden Angelica are long, spindle-shaped and fleshy—large specimens weighing sometimes as much as three pounds. The stems are stout, fluted, 4 to 6 feet high and hollow, the foliage is bold and pleasing, the leaves are on long, stout, hollow foot-stalks, often 3 feet in length, reddish purple at the clasping bases; the blades, of a bright green colour, are much cut into, being composed of numerous small leaflets, divided into three different groups, each of which is again subdivided into three lesser groups. The edges of the leaflets are finally toothed or serrated. The flowers, small and numerous, yellowish or greenish in colour, are grouped into large roundish umbels. They blossom in July and are succeeded by pale yellow, oblong fruits, with membraneous edges, flattened on one side and convex on the other, which bears three prominent ribs.

Our native plant, *Angelica sylvestris,* is hairy in stalk and stem to a degree which makes a well-marked difference. Its flowers differ, also, in being white. This variety is said to produce a good yellow dye.

Angelica is unique amongst the *Umbelliferæ,* with its pervading aromatic odour, a pleasant perfume, entirely differing from Fennel, Parsley, Anise, Caraway or Chervil. One old writer strangely compared it to Musk, others to Juniper. Even the roots are also fragrant.

In several London squares and parks, Angelica has continued to grow, self-sown, for several generations as a garden escape, often unrecognised by the multitude; in some it is appropriated as a useful foliage plant, in others it is treated rather as an intruding weed. Before the building of the London Law Courts and the clearing of much slum property between Holywell Street and Seven Dials, the foreign population of that district fully appreciated its value, and were always anxious to get it from Lincoln's Inn Fields, where it abounded and where it still grows. Until very recent years it was exceedingly common on the slopes bordering the Tower of London on the north and west sides; there also, the inhabitants held the plant in high repute for culinary use and for its hygienic merit.

CULTIVATION. Cultivate in ordinary deep moist loam, in a shaded position, as the plant thrives best in a damp soil and loves to grow near running water. Although its natural habitat is in damp soil and in open quarters, yet it can withstand adverse environment wonderfully well and even endure severe winter frost without harm. Seedlings will even successfully develop and flower under trees whose shelter creates an area of summer dryness in the surface soil, but, of course, though such conditions may be allowable when Angelica is grown merely as an ornamental plant, it must be given the best treatment as regards suitable soil when grown for its use commercially. Insects and garden pests do not attack the plant with much avidity; its worst enemy is a small two-winged fly, of which the maggots are leaf-miners, resembling those of the Celery plant and of the Spinach leaf.

PROPAGATION should not be attempted otherwise than by the sowing of ripe, fresh seed, though division of old roots is sometimes recommended, and also propagation by off-shoots, which are thrown out by a two-year plant when cut down in June for the sake of the stems, and which, trans-planted to 2 feet or more apart, will provide a quick method of propagation, considered inferior, however, to that of rais-ing by seed.

Since the germinating capacity of the seeds rapidly deterior-ates, they should be sown as soon as ripe in August or early September. If kept until March, especially if stored in paper packets, their vitality is likely to be seriously impaired. In the autumn the seeds may be sown where the plants are to remain, or preferably in a nursery bed, which as a rule will not need protection during the winter. A very slight cover-ing of earth is best. Young seedlings, but not the old plants, are amenable to transplantation. The seedlings should be transplanted when still small, for their first summer's growth to a distance of about 18 inches apart. In the autumn they can be removed to permanent quarters, the plants being then set 3 feet apart.

If well grown, the leaves may be cut for use the summer after transplanting. Ordinarily it is in the third or fourth year that the plant develops its tall flowering stem, of which the gathering for culinary or confectionery use prolongs the lifetime of the plant for many seasons. Unless it is desired to collect seed, the tops should be cut at or before flowering time. After producing seed the plants generally die, but by cutting down the tops when the flowerheads first appear and thus preventing the formation of seed, the plants may continue for several years longer. By cutting down the stems right at their base the plants practically become perennial, by the development of side shoots around the stool head.

If the seeds are required, they should be gathered when ripe and treated as described on page 18.

The stem, which is in great demand when trimmed and candied, should be cut about June or early July.

Uses. Angelica is largely used in the grocery trade as well as for medicine, and is a popular flavour for confectionery and liqueurs. The appreciation of its unique flavour was established in ancient times, when saccharin was extremely rare.

The preparation of Angelica is a small but important industry in the south of France, its cultivation being centralised in Clermont-Ferrand. Fairly large quantities are purchased by confectioners, and high prices are always easily obtainable. The flavour of Angelica distinctly suggests that of Juniper berries, as already mentioned, and it is largely used in combination with Juniper berries, or in partial substitution for them, by gin distillers. The stem is largely used in the preparation of preserved fruits and "confitures" generally, and is also used as an aromatic garnish by confectioners. The roots, leaves and seeds are used either in infusion or teas medicinally. The seeds, especially, which are aromatic and bitterish, are employed as alcoholic distillates, especially in the preparation of Vermouth and similar preparations, as well as in liqueurs, notably Chartreuse, and to a small extent in perfumery. From most ancient times, Angelica has been one of the chief flavouring ingredients of beverages and liqueurs, but probably it will be known only to a few people that the Muscatel Grape-like flavour of some wines made on both sides of the Rhine is (or is suspected to be) due to the secret use of Angelica. Essential oils are distilled in Germany, England, etc., from fruits and roots. They are expensive. Like the seeds, the oils are used for flavouring.

Though the tender leaflets, or blades of the leaves, have sometimes been recommended as a substitute for spinach, they are too bitter for the general taste, but the blanched mid-ribs of the leaf, boiled and used as a celery, are delicious, and Icelanders eat both the stem and the roots raw, with butter. The taste of the juicy raw stems is at first sweetish and slightly bitter in the mouth, and then gives a feeling of glowing warmth. The Finns eat the young stems baked in hot ashes, and an infusion of the dried herb is drunk either hot or cold: the flavour of the decoction is rather bitter, the colour is a pale-greenish grey, and the odour greatly resembles China tea. Another old practice is to put a portion of the herb into the pot in which fish is boiled.

The Norwegians make bread of the roots. The roots form one of the principal aromatics of European growth; the other parts of the plant have the same flavour, but their active principles are considered more perishable.

Gerarde says of Angelica: "If you do but take a piece of the root and hold it in your mouth, or chew the same between your teeth, it doth most certainly drive away pestilent aire."

If an incision is made in the bark of the stems and crown of the root, at the commencement of the spring, a resinous gum exudes, with aromatic flavour, similar to musk or benzoin, for either of which it can be substituted.

If a small quantity of the leaf-stalks of Angelica be cooked with "sticks" of Rhubarb, the flavour of the compound will be acceptable to many who do not relish plain Rhubarb. The quantity of Angelica used may be according to circumstances, conditions and individual taste. If the stems are young and juicy, they may be treated like Rhubarb and cut up small, the quantity used being any proportion between 5 and 25 per cent. If the stalks are more or less fully developed, or even rather old and tough, they can be excellently used in economically small quantities for flavouring large quantities of stewed Rhubarb, or Rhubarb jam, being added in long lengths before cooking and removed before sending to table. The confectioner's candied Angelica may be similarly utilised, but is extremely expensive and not so good, whilst the home-garden growth in spring time of fresh Angelica, with thick, stout leaf stalks and of still stouter flowering stems, is very easy and cheap. If this flowering stem be cut whilst very tender, early in May, later leaf-stalks will be plentifully available for use with the latter part of the Rhubarb crop.

The late Mr. Robertson, jam maker and confectioner of Chelsea, won considerable reputation by reason of his judicious blending of Angelica in jam making and its combination in other confections, including temperance beverages.

A pleasant form of hop bitters is made by taking 1oz. of dried Angelica herb, combined with 1oz. Holy Thistle and ½oz. Hops, infused with three pints of boiling water, and strained off when cold, a wineglassful being taken several times a day, before meals, and forming a good appetiser.

To PRESERVE ANGELICA. Cut in pieces 4ins. long, steep for twelve hours in salt and water. Put a layer of cabbage or cauliflower leaves in a clean brass pan, then a layer of Angelica, then another layer of leaves and so on, finishing with a layer of leaves on the top. Cover with water and vinegar. Boil slowly till the Angelica becomes quite green, then strain and weigh the stems. Allow 1lb. of loaf sugar to each pound of stems. Put the sugar on in a clean pan with water to cover; boil for ten minutes, and pour this syrup over the Angelica. Stand for twelve hours. Pour off the syrup, boil it up for five minutes and pour it again over the Angelica. Repeat the process, and after the Angelica has stood in the syrup twelve hours, put all on the fire in the brass pan and boil till tender. Then take out the pieces of Angelica, put them in a jar and pour the syrup over them, or dry them on a sieve and sprinkle them with sugar: they then form candy.

ANOTHER METHOD. Choose young stems, and cut them into suitable lengths (for commercial uses the stalks should be 15ins. long and secondary ones about 8ins.; they should be packed separately into bundles); then boil until tender; remove from the water, and take off the outer skin. After this has been done return to the water and let it simmer slowly until it becomes a good green. Dry the stems and weigh, allowing one pound of Angelica to each pound of sugar. Lay the boiled stalks in an earthenware pan and sprinkle the sugar over them, letting them stand for two days and then boil them. After boiling well, remove them from the fire and turn into a colander to drain away the superfluous syrup. Add more sugar and boil to syrup again, throwing in the Angelica; allow it to remain in the syrup for some minutes and then place singly in plates to dry off in a cool oven.

ANGELICA JAM. Choose tender stems of Angelica, cut them into fairly long strips, bleaching them in boiling water until they become soft. Then soak them in cold water for twelve hours. 1½lbs. of sugar will be needed to each 2lbs. of Angelica. First make the sugar into a syrup and put in the Angelica and cook until it is done. Afterwards put into pots in the usual way.

For Angelica used in wines, Herb beers, and liqueurs, see Part II—Wines, Herb Beers, and Liqueurs.

ANISE

(N.O. UMBELLIFERÆ)

PIMPINELLA ANISUM Linn.
> Local name: Anise.

ILLICIUM VERUM HK.f.
> Local names: Star-Anise; Chinese Anise; Aniseed Star, Badiane.

USES

The FRUIT or so-called SEEDS powdered as spice, used for flavouring soups, as an ingredient of various condiments, and medicinally; also used in preparation of liqueurs.

LEAVES, applied externally, are said to remove freckles. Also used in salad and as a pot-herb.

OIL as antiseptic, etc.

Anise is a little umbelliferous annual, highly valued as a cultivated crop prior to our era, both in Palestine and other parts of the East. It is a native of Egypt, Greece, Crete and Asia Minor, was cultivated by the ancient Egyptians and well known to the Greeks and Romans. Pliny tells us that "Both green and dried, it is held in high repute as an ingredient in all seasonings and sauces, and is also placed beneath the under-crust of bread." In the Middle Ages, its cultivation spread to Central Europe. In this country, Anise has been in use since the fourteenth century, and has been an inhabitant of English gardens from the middle of the sixteenth century, but it ripens its seeds here only in very warm summers, and it is chiefly in warmer countries that it is grown on a commercial scale, Southern Russia, Bulgaria, Germany, Malta, Spain, Italy, Greece and North Africa producing large quantities. It has also been introduced into India and South America. The cultivated plant attains a considerably larger size than the wild one.

Two of the species are natives in Britain, usually known as Burnet Saxifrage; they have no important properties.

DESCRIPTION. It is a dainty little plant, its slender stems about 18 inches high, erect, branched and cylindrical, arising from a white, spindle-shaped and rather fibrous root. Its root-leaves are lobed, somewhat like those of celery, but its stem-leaves are more and more finely cut towards the upper part of the stem, near the top of which their segments become very finely divided, like those of Fennel. Its flowers are small, of a yellowish white, in loose umbels formed of many umbellules. The fruits (popularly called "seeds") are greenish-grey, oblong in shape and furrowed and ridged, of an aromatic and agreeable odour and sweet and spicy taste.

Star-anise belongs to the natural order Magnoliaceæ, and is a small evergreen tree very like the laurel. The fruit grows in the form of a star, hence its name.

A similar, but poisonous, species is found in Japan.

CULTIVATION. Sow the seed, which should be as fresh as possible, never more than two years old, in dry, light soil, on a warm, sunny border, early in April, where the plants are to remain. When they are about two inches high, thin them, allowing about a foot each way. The seeds may also be sown in pots in heat, and removed to a warm site in May, but the plants do not transplant readily.

When planting on a commercial scale, sow in drills, 15 to 18 inches apart, and thin out to six inches apart in the rows. An ounce of seed should plant about 150 feet of drills, if the seeds are sown about half-inch apart. A light application of well-rotted manure, careful preparation of the ground, and keeping free from weeds are all that is required.

The seeds will ripen in England in good seasons if planted in a warm and favourable situation, though not successful everywhere, and can hardly be looked upon as a remunerative crop. The plant flowers in July, and if the season prove warm, will ripen in autumn, in about four months from the sowing of the seed, and in about one month from the appearance of the flowers, when the plants are cut down and the seeds threshed out.

Uses. In Virgil's time, Anise was used as a spice. Mustacæ, or spiced cakes of the Romans, introduced at the end of a rich meal to prevent indigestion, consisted of meal, with Anise, Cummin, and other aromatics. Such a cake was sometimes brought in at the end of a marriage feast, and is, perhaps, the origin of our spiced wedding cake.

On the Continent, especially in Germany, many cakes have an aniseed flavouring, and Anise is also used in a flavouring for soups, and is an ingredient of various condiments, especially curry powders, and is also used to flavour some kinds of cheese and bread.

The ground seeds also form one of the ingredients of sachet powders.

Anise fruit yields on distillation a fragrant, syrupy, volatile oil, that is nearly colourless, about 50lbs. of seed being required to produce 1lb. of oil. It is largely employed in France, Spain, Italy and South America in the preparation of cordial liqueurs. The liqueur Anisette, made by mixing the oil with spirits of wine, added to cold water on a hot summer's day, is a most refreshing drink.

Anise oil is a good antiseptic, and is used mixed with oil of Peppermint or Wintergreen to flavour aromatic liquid dentifrices. It is also mixed with other fluids for liquid perfumes, and largely used in perfuming soaps, pomatums, and other toilet articles.

The oil is said to prove a capital bait for mice, if smeared in traps. It is poisonous to pigeons. It destroys lice and the itch insect, it being mixed with lard for the purpose and made into an ointment.

At Erfurt, in Germany, where much of the commercial oil is made, the whole plant and the seeds are both used for distilling.

The powdered seed is largely used in condition pills and other condiments for horses.

The leaves have frequently been employed as a garnish for flavouring salads, and to a limited extent as a pot-herb.

For Anise used in liqueur, see Part II.

BALM

(N.O. LABIATÆ)

MELISSA OFFICINALIS Linn.
Local Names: Balm, Sweet Balm, Lemon Balm.

USES

THE FOLIAGE is widely used for flavouring soups, stews, sauces, and dressings, and, when fresh, to a small extent with salads.

STEMS AND LEAVES still used occasionally in medicine.

FRUITS for liqueurs and cordials.

Balm, also known as Sweet Balm and Lemon Balm, is a well-known perennial plant belonging to the order *Labiatæ*.

The word Balm is an abbreviation of Balsam, the chief of sweet-smelling oils. It is so called from its honied sweetness. The generic name Melissa is Greek for bee, given it in allusion to the fondness of bees for the abundant nectar stored in its flowers. Gerarde says: "It is profitably planted where bees are kept. The hives of bees being rubbed with the leaves of bawme, causeth the bees to keep together, and causeth others to come with them." And again, quoting Pliny: "When they are strayed away, they do find their way home by it."

It is a native of Southern Europe, where over 2,000 years ago it was cultivated as a source of honey and as sweet herb, and it is frequently mentioned in the Greek and Latin classics. It has been introduced as a garden plant into nearly all temperate climates.

Description. The root-stock is short, the roots small and fibrous; the stem, square and branching, grows 1-2ft. high, and has at each joint pairs of broadly heart-shaped, toothed leaves, which emit a fragrant lemon odour when bruised. They also have a distinct lemon taste. The flowers, white or yellowish, are in loose, small, one-sided clusters from the axils of the leaves, and bloom from June to October. The plant dies down in winter, but the root is perennial. The seeds are very small, more than 50,000 to the ounce.

Cultivation. Balm grows freely in any soil and can be propagated by seeds sown in May, and by cuttings or division of roots in spring or autumn; if in autumn, preferably not later than October, so that the offsets may be established before the frosts come on. The roots may be divided into small pieces, with three or four buds to each, and planted two feet apart in ordinary garden soil. The only culture required is to keep them free from weeds and to cut off the decayed stalks in autumn, and then to stir the ground between the roots.

The seeds germinate fairly well, even when four years old. Owing to their small size, they should be planted in a seed-pan in a greenhouse in very fine and friable soil, on the surface of which they are merely pressed. When an inch tall, they should be pricked out 2ins. apart in shallow boxes, and when 4ins. tall set out in the open, in rows 18ins. apart and 1ft. apart in the rows. When once established, they may be increased readily by cuttings, layers, or division of roots.

The foliage of seedling plants, or plants spring set, should be ready for use by midsummer; that of established plants from early spring until late autumn.

A variety of the common Catmint (*Nepeta Cataria*) is sometimes mistaken for Balm—its smell is very like it. A native of the South of England and also found in several parts of Europe is *Melittis Melissophyllum,* called Bastard Balm. This is very beautiful, and when dried is of a wonderful fragrance and this fragrance is retained for a considerable period. In America *Calamintha Nepeta* is very often called Field Balm and *Collinsonia* is known as Horse Balm. A large number of the *Labiatæ* family have balm-like properties.

For home use and market, the foliage should be dried as directed, but the more succulent stems not in bunches over strings, but laid on trays or sieves, thinly spread. The temperature should be rather low.

To make Balm Tea, pour one pint of boiling water on 1oz. of herb, infuse 15 minutes, allow to cool, then strain, and drink freely.

See Part II for details of the fruit used in liqueurs.

BASIL

(N.O. Labiatæ)

Ocimum Basilicum Linn.
Local name: Sweet Basil.
Ocimum minimum Linn.
Local name: Bush Basil.

USES

The Foliage furnishes oil and is used as flavouring for soups, and is also used in ragouts and sauces. Leafy tops used in salads and cups. The oil is also used in perfumery. Also occasionally used medicinally.

Common or Sweet Basil, which is used in medicine and also for culinary purposes, especially in France, is an annual, belonging to the order *Labiatæ*. The plant is a native of tropical Asia, where for centuries, especially in India, it has been highly esteemed as a condiment. It was introduced into England about the middle of the sixteenth century.

The derivation of the name Basil is uncertain. Some say it comes from the Greek *basileus*, a king, for some reason unknown, unless as Parkinson says, because "the smell thereof is so excellent that it is fit for a king's house," or it may have been termed royal, because used of old in some regal unguent, or bath, or medicine.

In France it is known as Herbe Royale, royal herb. The generic name is derived from Oza, a Greek word signifying odour.

Boccaccio's story of Isabella and the Pot of Basil, immortal-ised for us by the pen of Keats and the brush of Rossetti, keeps the plant in our memory, though it is now somewhat rarely seen cultivated in this country. It was formerly a more frequent denizen of English herb gardens, for Tusser includes it among the Strewing herbs, and Drayton places is first in order, when enumerating the herbs in his poem *Polyolbion*.

> "With Basil then I will begin
> Whose scent is wondrous pleasing."

In Tudor days, little pots of Basil were often given as graceful compliments by farmers' wives to their landladies and to visitors. Parkinson says of it: "The ordinary Basil is in a manner wholly spent to make sweete or washing waters among other sweet herbs, yet sometimes it is put into nosegays. The Physicall properties are to procure a cheerfull and merry hearte whereunto the seeds is chiefly used in powder."

The ancients had many superstitions connected with Basil, among which was the belief that it had the power of propagating scorpions. *Chambers' Encyclopædia* says:—

"The belief that it thrives especially on the brains of murdered men occurs in the *Decameron,* and is rendered familiar by Holman Hunt's picture."

DESCRIPTION. Sweet Basil is a hairy plant growing about 3ft. high. The stem is obtusely quadrangular, the labiate flowers are white, in whorls in the axils of the leaves, the calyx with the upper lobe rounded and spreading. The leaves, greyish-green beneath and dotted with dark oil cells, are opposite, 1in. long and one-third inch broad, stalked and peculiarly smooth, soft and cool to the touch, very slightly toothed, and if slightly bruised exale a very delightful scent of cloves.

There are several varieties, different in the size, shape, odour and colour of the leaves. The Common Basil has very dark green leaves, the curled-leaved has short spikes of flowers, the narrow-leaved smells like Fennel, another has a scent of citron, another somewhat of a Tarragon scent. Lettuce-leaved Basil has large pale-green, wrinkled leaves like those of lettuce; Purple Basil has lilac flowers, and, grown in strong sun, purple leaf-stems and young branches.

CULTIVATION. Basil dies down every year in this country, so that the seeds have to be sown annually. If in a very warm sheltered spot, seeds may be sown in the open, about the last week in April, but they are a long time coming up, and as they are very small (about 23,000 to the ounce) it is preferable to sow in a hot bed, about the end of March, and remove to a warm border in May, planting 10ins. to a foot apart. Basil flourishes best in a rich soil and sunny situation.

First gatherings of foliage should begin by mid-summer, when the plant starts to blossom. Then they may be cut to within a few inches of the ground. A second or even a third crop may be obtained if care is taken to keep the surface clean and open. A little dressing of quickly available fertiliser applied at the time is helpful. Some of the best plants should be left uncut for seed, which should ripen by mid-summer.

For winter use of the fresh leaves, plants may be transplanted from the garden into frames, or seedlings may be started in September. The seeds should be sown two to the inch and the seedlings transplanted to pots or boxes, in the latter 5 or 6ins. apart each way.

Basil is chiefly used fresh, but may also be dried in the manner already described, being gathered in July, and stored dry for winter use.

In common with other labiates, Basil, both the wild and the sweet, furnishes an aromatic, volatile, camphoraceous oil, and on this account is much employed in France for flavouring soups, especially turtle soup, which derives its peculiar taste chiefly from the clove-like flavour of Basil. The French also use it in ragouts and sauces. The leafy tops are a great improvement to salads and cups.

Although it is now comparatively little used in England for culinary purposes, this herb was one of our favourite potherbs in olden days, and was employed for giving the distinctive flavour that once made Fetter Lane sausages famous.

The golden-yellow essential oil, which is extracted from the leaves, is used in perfumery more than in the kitchen.

Bush Basil, *Ocimum minimum,* is a low bushy plant, seldom above 6ins. in height, much smaller and more compact than Sweet Basil.

The leaves are ovate, quite entire, the flowers in whorls towards the top of the branches, smaller than those of Sweet Basil, and seldom succeeded by ripe seeds in England.

There are two varieties, one with dark purple leaves and the other with variable leaves.

Bush Basil may occasionally live through the winter in this country, though Sweet Basil never does.

Both varieties flower in July and August.

The leafy tops of Bush Basil are used in the same manner as the Sweet Basil for seasoning and in salads.

Basil Thyme (*Calamintha Acinos*) is native to Britain and is quite as fragrant.

Basil Vinegar is made in the same way as Mint Vinegar, that is, by steeping the leaves in vinegar. When the fresh plant is unobtainable in the winter, this can be used in its place for flavouring purposes.

From *Speculum Mundi*:—

"First, concerning herbs, I begin with Basil, whose seeds, being mixed with shoemakers' black, do take away warts. We in England, though we seldom eat it, yet greatly do esteem it because it smelleth sweet, and comforteth the brain."

BAY LAUREL

(N.O. Lauraceæ)

Laurus nobilis Linn.
    Local name: Bay Laurel.

USES

Leaves for culinary purposes as a flavouring, and used by perfumers.

The foliage of the Sweet Bay or Bay Laurel (*Laurus Nobilis*) which is in this country only a large, hardy shrub, but in Southern Europe becomes a tree, 20–30ft. in height, is very aromatic, and is much used for culinary purposes, for flavouring soups, stews, sardines, figs, etc.

At one time it was only the fruit which was called "Bay," but at the present time the name is given to the whole plant. The hardy evergreen which is so often used in shrubberies —the Common Laurel—is by some called "Bay Laurel." The true Bay leaves are used for flavouring puddings, etc., and sometimes those of the Laurel are used as a substitute.

Care must be exercised not to use in error the leaves of the Cherry Laurel, which have sometimes been mistaken for those of the Bay Laurel, for flavouring, with disastrous results; they produce prussic acid, and the water distilled from them is a virulent poison.

An oil is expressed from the berries of the Sweet Bay (*Oleum Lauri expressum*), used medicinally as a local application for Rheumatism, and the volatile oil is employed to communicate a pleasant odour to external remedies. An infusion was also formerly made of the leaves and berries as a stomachic, but they are now rarely used internally as medicines.

In classic days, when the people crowded into Rome during the time of the Italian plague, they were all recommended to go to Laurentinum (now San Lorenzo) because the Sweet Bay there grew in great abundance, and the inhalation of air impregnated with its odours was considered a sure prevention against infection.

The essential Oil of Bay is not distilled from the Sweet Bay, but from the fresh leaves of *Pimenta acris,* a native of the West Indies. It is not used internally, but solely for the purpose of making Bay Rum and Florida Water for toilet articles.

In olden times Bay leaves were used to decorate the house at Christmas and for weddings. If a Bay tree withered it was thought to foretell an evil happening. The ancients wore Bay leaves as a protection against thunder.

The following passage is taken from Parkinson's *Garden of Flowers,* 1629:—

"The Bay leaves are of as necessary use as any other in the garden or orchard, for they serve both for pleasure and profit, both for ornament and for use, both for honest civil uses and for physic, yea, both for the sick and the sound, both for the living and the dead; . . . so that from the cradle to the grave we still have use of it, we still have need of it."

BORAGE

(N.O. BORAGINACEÆ)

BORAGOFFICINALIS Linn.
   Local name: Borage.

USES

YOUNG LEAVES used in pickles and salad.
LEAVES used in Claret Cup.
STEM and LEAVES supply much saline mucilage.
FLOWERS dried for mixing with Pot Pourri.

The Common Borage is a hardy annual plant, coming originally from Aleppo, but now naturalised in most parts of Europe and frequently found in this country, though mostly only on rubbish-heaps and near dwellings, and generally to be regarded as a garden escape. It belongs to the order of Boraginaceæ.

It has long been grown freely in kitchen gardens, both for its uses as a herb and for the sake of its flowers, of which bees are very fond, as it yields much excellent honey.

From *English Wild Flowers,* by J. T. Burgess:—

"The grey leaves of the sullen-looking Borage (*Boragofficinalis*) rear themselves in out-of-the-way places. The rough foliage hides its azure flowers, whose white eyes are in direct contrast to the prominent purple stamens. Rough as this borage is, but few plants have been more popular. Its young shoots have been eaten with salad and pickled. Its leaves form still an ingredient in 'claret cup' and 'cool tankard.' Formerly every gardener cultivated it; now its glory is departed, a few plants only being kept near the apiary for the bees."

Description. The whole plant is rough, with white, stiff, prickly hairs. The round stems, about a foot and a half high, are branched, hollow and succulent; the leaves, alternate, large, wrinkled, deep green, oval and pointed, 3ins. long or more, and about 1½ins. broad, the lower ones stalked, with stiff, one-celled hairs on the upper surfaces and on the veins below, the margins entire, but wavy. The flowers are bright blue and star-shaped, distinguished from those of every plant in this order by their prominent black anthers, which form a cone in the centre and have been described as their beauty spot. The fruit consists of four brownish-black nutlets. The seeds retain their vitality for about eight years. The flowers are sometimes pink, violet-red, and even white.

Cultivation. Borage flourishes in ordinary soil, and no plant is more easily grown. It may be propagated by division of root-stocks in spring, and by putting cuttings of shoots in sandy soil in a cold frame in summer and autumn, or from seeds sown in fairly good, light soil, from the middle of March to May, in drills 18ins. apart, the seedlings being thinned out to about 15ins. apart in the rows. If left alone, Borage will seed itself freely and comes up year after year in the same place. Seeds may also be sown in the autumn. Those sown then will flower in May, whereas those sown in the spring will not flower till June.

The fresh herb has a cucumber-like fragrance. When steeped in water, it imparts a coolness to it and also a faint cucumber flavour, and compounded with lemon and sugar in wine, with water, it makes a refreshing and restorative summer drink. It was formerly always an ingredient in cool tankards of wine and cider, and is still largely used in claret cup.

Our great-grandmothers preserved the flowers and candied them.

In the early part of the nineteenth century, the young tops of Borage were still sometimes boiled as a potherb, and the young leaves were formerly considered good in salads.

Gerarde tells us: "Pliny calls it Euphrosinum, because it maketh a man merry and joyful: which thing also the old verse concerning Borage doth testifie:

Ego Borago   I, Borage
Gaudia semper ago.   Bring alwaies courage.

"Those of our time do use the flowers in sallads to exhilerate and make the mind glad. There be also many things made of these used everywhere for the comfort of the heart, for the driving away of sorrow and increasing the joy of the minde. The leaves and floures of Borage put into wine make men and women glad and merry and drive away all sadnesse, dulnesse and melancholy, as Dioscorides and Pliny affirme. Syrup made of the floures of Borage comforteth the heart, purgeth melancholy and quieteth the phrenticke and lunaticke person. The leaves eaten raw ingender good blood, especially in those that have been lately sicke." The stems and leaves supply much saline mucilage, which when boiled and cooked, likewise deposits nitre and common salt. It is to these saline qualities that the wholesome invigorating effects and specially recruiting properties of Borage are supposed to be due, as they promote the activity of the kidneys.

Borage flowers are also dried for mixing with Pot Pourri, mainly for the sake of their bright blue colour. They should be collected as early as possible before expansion, but when fully formed, otherwise they soon lose their colour, and must not be allowed to lie in heaps before drying. Lay them on trays in thin layers in a current of air as soon as possible after gathering.

The flowers of Borage used also to be put into salads, both as a decoration and for their cucumber flavour.

BURNET
(N.O. ROSACEÆ)

POTERIUM SANGUISORBA Linn.
Local name: Burnet or Lesser Burnet.

USES

YOUNG LEAVES for salad and also for cool tankards in the same way as Borage.

The Garden or Salad Burnet, a member of the natural order *Rosaceæ,* is assigned to the genus *Poterium,* which name is derived "poterion" a drinking cup, from the use to which its leaves were applied in the preparation of the numerous beverages with which the "poterion" was filled in ancient times.

It is common in dry pastures and by the wayside, especially on chalk and limestone, but is rarer in Scotland and Ireland than in England.

DESCRIPTION. The Salad Burnet is an elegant little plant, its stems rising about a foot high, its leaves being on long stalks bearing five to ten pairs of sharply-toothed leaflets. The flowers are in oblong heads, on long stalks, with four-toothed, coloured membraneous calyces, with crimson tufted stigmas, and the lower ones with 30 to 40 stamens, having very long drooping filaments. Both the flower and leaf-stalks are of deep crimson colour.

From *English Wild Flowers* (J. T. Burgess):—

"In July, on dry chalky pastures, the dull purplish-red flowers of the Salad Burnet (*Poterium Sanguisorba*) may be found. The flowers grow on a stem some 2ft. high. The egg-shaped serrated leaflets are numerous, and have the taste and scent of cucumber, and are frequently eaten in salads, though the flavour is somewhat hot. When the anthers appear the flower becomes conspicuous, as they are very numerous, and hairy around the head.

"The Great Burnet (*Sanguisorba officinalis*) is more frequent in the Northern Counties in moist meadows. The stem is from 1 to 3ft. in height. The dark purple flowers are much crowded on its oval head. Its old name of Bloodwort pointed to its real or supposed use as a styptic."

CULTIVATION. It is easily propagated by seeds, sown in autumn, soon after they are ripe. If the seeds be permitted to scatter, the plants will come up plentifully, and can be transplanted into an ordinary or rather poor soil, at about a foot distant each way. If kept clear from weeds, they will continue some years without further care, especially if the soil be dry. Propagation may also be effected by division of roots in spring or autumn.

When used for salad, the flower-stalks should be cut down if not required for seed. The leaves, for salad uses, should be cut young, or may be tough.

In the herb gardens of older days, the Salad Burnet always had its place. Bacon recommends it to be set in alleys, together with wild thyme and water mint, to perfume the air most delightfully, being trodden on and crushed.

The leaves when bruised smell like cucumber and taste somewhat like it, and from this property it was reckoned

49

among the salad herbs and used to be put into cool tankards in the same manner as Borage, though it has gone out of fashion and as a kitchen-herb is now much neglected.

Turner advised the use of the herb, infused in wine or beer. The Italians and French call the Burnet "Pimpinella." In Italy it has passed into a proverb:—

> "L'Insalata non e buon, ne bella
> Ove non e la Pimpinella.
>
> That salad is neither good nor fair,
> If Pimpinella is not there."

BURNET VINEGAR. Take a quart of vinegar and pour it over half an ounce of well-dried and pounded Burnet seed. Pour it into a bottle and cork tightly. Shake the bottle well once a day for 10 days; strain and cork tightly—it will then be ready for use.

CARAWAY

(N.O. UMBELLIFERÆ)

CARUM CARVI Linn.
Local name: Caraway.

USES

FRUITS as a flavouring in cookery, confectionery, and liqueurs.

LEAVES possess an oil identical with that of the fruit but not made use of. The leaves have been boiled in soup as an aromatic flavouring, and occasionally leaves and young shoots have been used as an ingredient in salads.

ROOTS, edible.

Caraway is another member of the group of aromatic, umbelliferous plants characterised by having carminative properties, like Anise, Cumin, Dill and Fennel. It is grown, however, less for the medicinal properties of the fruits, or so-called "seeds," than for their use as a flavouring material in cookery, confectionery and liqueurs.

The plant is distributed throughout the northern and central parts of Europe and Asia, though where it occurs in this country it is only considered a naturalised species, having apparently escaped cultivation.

Caraway was well known in far-off classic days, and it is believed that its use originated with the ancient Arabs, who called the "seeds" *Karawaya,* a name they still bear in the East, and clearly the origin of our word Caraway.

DESCRIPTION. It is a biennial, with smooth, furrowed stems, growing $1\frac{1}{2}$ to 2ft. high, bearing finely-cut leaves, and umbels of white flowers which blossom in June. The fruits—which are popularly and incorrectly called seeds—and which correspond in general character to those of the other plants of this large family, are laterally compressed, somewhat horny and translucent, slightly curved, and marked with five distinct, pale ridges. They evolve a pleasant, aromatic odour when bruised, and have an agreeable taste.

The leaves possess similar properties and afford an oil identical with that of the fruit, though it is not made use of.

CULTIVATION. Caraway does best when the seeds are sown in the autumn, as soon as ripe, though they may be sown in March. Sow in drills, 1ft. apart, the plants when strong enough being thinned out to about 8ins. in the rows. The ground will require an occasional hoeing to keep it clean and assist the growth of the plants. From an autumn-sown crop, seeds will be produced in the following summer, ripening about August.

When the fruit ripens the plants are cut about 12ins. above the ground with sickles, and the caraways are separated by threshing. They can be dried either on trays in the sun or by very gentle heat over a stove, shaking occasionally.

Although Caraway is indigenous to all parts of Europe, Siberia, Turkey in Asia, Persia, India and North Africa, yet it is cultivated only in a few comparatively restricted areas. It grows wild in many parts of Canada and the United States, but is nowhere grown there as a field or garden crop. Its cultivation is restricted to relatively small areas in England, Holland, Germany, Finland, Russia, Norway and Morocco, where it constitutes one of the chief agricultural industries within its narrow confines. It has so far received comparatively little attention in England, where it is grown only in Essex, Kent and Suffolk, upon old grass land broken up for the purpose. Holland cultivates the main crop, producing and exporting far larger quantities than any other country.

Dutch Caraway is preferred among consumers in the United States, and the bulk used there comes from Holland. Morocco produces a grade of Caraway that comes regularly into the English and American markets, but is somewhat inferior in quality. During the last year or two there has been a scarcity of Caraway, owing partly to the fact that the extensive area of land in Holland usually employed for the cultivation of the plant was devastated by floods towards the close of 1915. Moreover, the exportation of Caraway from Holland was forbidden. The cultivation of Caraway plants has therefore been advised as likely to be profitable, as on account of the ruling scarcity the price of Caraway seed became double what it was before the war. Much Dill seed was sold in its place, especially Indian Dill seed. In 1918, a small grower reported that she had netted £5 from growing

Caraway on a corner of what otherwise would have been waste ground.

The tender leaves in spring have been boiled in soup to give it an aromatic flavour, and occasionally the leaves and young shoots have been used as an ingredient in salads.

The roots are thick and tapering, like a parsnip, though much smaller and are edible. Parkinson declared them, when young, to be superior in flavour to Parsnips. Mixed with milk and made into bread, they are said to have formed the "Chara" of Julius Cæsar, eaten by the soldiers of Valerius. It is the seeds, however, that are the important part.

Caraway is frequently mentioned by the old writers. In the Middle Ages and in Shakespeare's time it was very popular, and was more freely used in this country than in our own days. "The seed," says Parkinson, "is much used to be put among baked fruit, or into bread, cakes, etc., to give them a relish. It is also made into comfites and taken for cold or wind in the body, which also are served to the table with fruit." In *Henry IV*, Second Part, Squire Shallot invites Falstaff to "a pippin and a dish of caraways." The custom of serving roast apples with a little saucerful of Caraway is still kept up at Trinity College, Cambridge, and at some of the old-fashioned London Livery Dinners, just as in Shakespeare's days—and in Scotland to this day a saucerful is put down at tea to dip the buttered side of bread into and called "salt water jelly." I have not yet come across the reason of its getting this name.

The scattering of the seed over cakes has long been practised, and Caraway-seed cake was formerly a standing institution at the feasts given by farmers to their labourers at the end of the wheat sowing. The little Caraway comfits consist merely of the seeds encrusted with white sugar. In Germany, the peasants flavour their cheese, cabbage soups, and household bread with Caraway, and in Norway and Sweden, polenta-like, black, Caraway bread is largely eaten in country districts, and is delicious.

The oil extracted from the fruits is used as an ingredient of alcoholic liqueurs: both the Russians and the Germans make from Caraway a liqueur, "Kümmel," and Caraway enters into the composition of *l'huile de Vénus* and other cordials.

From 6lbs. of the unbruised seeds, 4ozs. of the pure essential oil can be expressed.

The exhausted seed, after the distillation of the oil, contains a high percentage of protein and fat, and is used as a cattle food.

Both fruit and oil possess aromatic, stimulant and carminative properties.

The flavour of the oil differs slightly in different varieties, the North Russian being preferred for the preparation of Kümmel, while the oil distilled from the Tunis variety of Caraway is of less pleasant flavour than the Dutch and English Caraways, and is mainly used for perfuming soaps, such as Brown Windsor soap.

A CONTINENTAL RECIPE

Two parts of beetroot that has lain in vinegar, one part sliced apple, one part sliced boiled potatoes, one teaspoonful chopped Horse-radish, flavoured with a pinch of pepper, a pinch of Caraway seeds, and a pinch of coriander.

(For Caraway used in liqueurs, see Part II.)

CATMINT

(N.O. Labiatæ)

Nepeta Cataria Linn.
Local Names: Catmint, Catnep.

USES

Flowering Tops used in medicine—dried.
The Plant is also used for bee forage.

Catmint or Catnep, a wild English plant belonging to the large family *Labiatæ,* is generally distributed throughout the central and the southern counties of England, in hedgerows, borders of fields, and on dry banks and waste ground, especially in chalky and gravelly soil. It is less common in the north, very local in Scotland and rare in Ireland, but of frequent occurrence in the whole of Europe and temperate Asia, and also common in North America, where originally, however, it was an introduced species.

Description. The root is perennial and sends up square, erect and branched stems, 2–3ft. high, which are very leafy and covered with a mealy down. The heart-shaped, toothed leaves are also covered with a soft, close down, especially on the under-sides, which are quite white with it, so that the whole plant has a hoary, greyish appearance, as though it had had dust blown all over it.

The flowers grow on short footstalks in dense whorls, which towards the summit of the stem are so close as almost to form a spike. They are in bloom from July to September. The individual flowers are small, the corollas two-lipped, the upper lip straight, of a whitish or pale pink colour, dotted with red spots, the anthers a deep red colour. The calyx tube

55

has 15 ribs, a distinguishing feature of the genus *Nepeta*, to which this species belongs.

The plant has an aromatic, characteristic odour, which bears a certain resemblance to that of both Mint and Pennyroyal. It is owing to this scent that it has a strange fascination for cats, who are so fond of the odour of this herb that they will destroy any plant of it that may happen to be bruised, so as to emit its peculiar pungent scent, rolling on it, tearing it to pieces and chewing it with the greatest pleasure, seeming to delight in the scent almost as much as in that of Valerian.

CULTIVATION. Catmint is easily grown in any garden soil, and does not require moisture in the same way as the other Mints. Seeds can be sown either in autumn or spring, where the plants are to remain, thinning out the seedlings to about 20ins. apart each way. They require no attention, and will last for several years if the ground is kept free from weeds. The germinating power of the seeds lasts five years. The stock may also easily be increased by dividing the plants in spring.

The herb was formerly in popular use, especially for flavouring sauces, but it has fallen into disuse in this country as a culinary herb, though in France, the leaves and young shoots are still much used for seasoning, and it is regularly grown amongst kitchen herbs for the purpose. But there, in this country and America, it has an old reputation for its value as a tea. Catmint tea, infused from the dried herb, is stimulating.

The flowering tops are harvested when the plant is in full bloom in August, and dried.

The most important use of the plant, however, is as a bee forage, for which purpose waste places are often planted with it.

CHERVIL

(N.O. Umbelliferæ)

Anthriscus Cerefolium Hoffm.
Local Name: Chervil.

USES

Leaves, used for seasoning, in mixed salads, and in soups; also for a garnish in the same way as parsley.

Chervil is an umbelliferous plant, which has long been cultivated as a pot-herb, more on the Continent than in Britain. The leaves have a rather sweet, aromatic smell and taste—rather unusual—and by this it may be distinguished from its relation *Anthriscus Scandix (Anthriscus vulgaris)*, which is very poisonous and has a very unpleasant smell, and another outstanding feature—its rough, bristly fruit.

Description. It has stems about 18ins. tall, bearing a few bright green leaves, composed of oval, much cut-into leaflets. The small white flowers, borne in umbels, are followed by long, pointed, black fruits, with a conspicuous furrow from end to end.

Cultivation. The culture is a very simple matter. The seeds, which retain their germinating power for about three years, may be sown in any ordinary garden soil in a sunny part of the garden, nearly all the year round. The leaves are ready to gather in six to eight weeks from the time of sowing. A winter supply may be obtained by sowing the seed in shallow boxes in a frame or cool greenhouse. Sow where the plants are to grow, as a rule, and do not transplant, merely thinning out, when sufficiently advanced, to 9ins. apart.

Gather the leaves when 3 or 4ins. high, and cut off close to the root, when they will shoot up again.

Small and frequent sowings are made at any time between the end of February and October, but a shadier position must be chosen in hot weather, and watering is necessary during the summer.

The tender leaves, which are highly aromatic, are used both in this country and in France for seasoning, and in mixed salads, also in soups. Chervil is rarely used alone, but is the chief ingredient in what the French call FINES HERBES, the mixture which enters into many culinary preparations.

The best variety is the Curled, which, having the same flavour, is a prettier garnish than the ordinary Chervil, and is used in this manner like Parsley, but fades more quickly.

The SWEET CICELY, or Giant Sweet Chervil (*Myrrhis odorata*) must not be confounded with the Common Chervil. It is a native of Great Britain, found in mountainous pastures in the North, and is a perennial, with a thick root (which used to be boiled and eaten with oil and vinegar) and very aromatic foliage, and was used in olden days as a salad herb.

The *Myrrhis odorata* is often cultivated in Germany, and called Anise Chervil or Spanish Chervil; Myrrh is its popular name in Scotland. Some people imagine that the smell is attractive to bees, and when swarms have been wanted to enter the hives, the insides of the hives have been impregnated with the smell of the leaves.

Gerarde writes of the Sweet Cicely thus:—

"It hath leaves of a very good and pleasant smell and taste like unto Chervil and something hairy, which has caused us to call it Sweet Chervil. The leaves of the Sweet Chervil are exceedingly good, wholesome, and pleasant among other sallad herbs, giving the taste of anise seed unto the rest. The seeds, eaten as a salad while they are yet green, with oyle, vinegar and pepper exceed all other sallads by many degrees, both in pleasantness of taste and sweetness of smell and wholesomeness for the cold and feeble stomachs. The roots are likewise most excellent in a salad with oil and vinegar, being first boiled, which is very good for old people that are dull and without courage."

The seeds were used to scent and polish oak floors and furniture in the North of England.

CHIVES

(N.O. Liliaceæ)

Allium Schœnoprasum Linn.
Local Name: Chives.

USES

Bulb, used as a substitute for Onions—both cooked and pickled; also used chopped up in salads.
"Grass" used in salads.

In England, Chives are comparatively little known, being by no means considered indispensable denizens of the kitchen garden, though in Scotland they are found in many a cottage garden and in France, where the science of cookery is more regarded than with us, they are very commonly used.

The Chive is the smallest, though one of the finest-flavoured of the Onion tribe, belonging to the botanical

E

group of plants that goes under the name of *Allium*, which includes also the Garlic, Leek and Shallot, and is part of the great order *Liliaceæ*.

Though said to be a native of Britain, it is only very rarely found here growing in an uncultivated state, and then only in the northern and western counties of England and Wales; where occasionally found wild in fields and meadows, it is generally only an outcast from the kitchen-garden. But it grows in rocky pastures throughout temperate and northern Europe.

DESCRIPTION. The plant is a hardy perennial; that is to say, produces each year fresh leaves from the same root, which is a tiny succulent bulb that lives through the winter under the surface of the ground after the leaves have died down in the autumn. The bulbs grow very close together in dense tufts or clusters, and are of an elongated form, with white, rather firm sheaths, the outer sheath sometimes grey.

The slender leaves appear early in spring and are long, cylindrical and hollow, tapering to a point and about the thickness of a crow-quill. They grow from 6 to 10ins. high.

The flowering stem is usually nipped off with cultivated plants (which are grown solely for the sake of the leaves, or "grass"), but when allowed to rise, it seldom reaches more than a few inches to at most a foot in height. It is hollow and either has no leaf at all on it, or has one leaf sheathing it below the middle. It supports a close globular head, or umbel, of purple flowers; the numerous flowers are densely packed together on separate, very slender little flower-stalks (botanically termed pedicels), shorter than the flowers themselves, which lengthen slightly as the fruit ripens, causing the heads to assume a conical instead of a round shape. The petals of the flowers are nearly half an inch long; when dry, their pale purple colour, which has in parts a darker flush, changes to rose colour. The anthers (the pollen-bearing part of the flower) are of a bluish-purple colour. The seed-vessel, or capsule, is a little larger than a hemp seed and is completely concealed within the petals, which are about twice its length. The small seeds which it contains are black when ripe and similar to Onion seeds.

The flowers are in blossom in June and July, and in the most cold and moist situations will mature their seeds, though rarely allowed to do so under cultivation.

Cultivation. The Chive will grow in any ordinary garden soil. It can be raised from seed, but is usually propagated by dividing the clumps in spring or autumn. In dividing the clumps, leave about six little bulbs together in a tiny clump, which will spread to a fine clump in the course of a year, and may then be divided. Set the clumps from 9ins. to a foot apart each way. For a quick return propagation by division of the bulb clumps is always to be preferred.

The green from the clumps can be cut three or four times in the season. When required for use, each clump may be cut in turn, fairly close to the ground. The leaves will soon grow again and be found more tender each time of cutting. By carefully cropping, the "grass" can be obtained quite late in the season, until the early frosts come, when it withers up and disappears through the winter, pushing up again in the first warm days of February. For early crops, a little "grass" can be forced on the clumps by placing cloches or a "light" over them.

Beyond weeding between the clumps, no further care or attention is needed after division. Beds should be re-planted at least once in three or four years.

If it is desired to produce seed, grow two plantations, one for producing "grass" for use, and the other to be left to flower and set seed, as you cannot get the two crops—"grass" and seed, off the one set of plants.

For market, the clumps are cut in squares and the whole plant sold. Treated thus, the greengrocers can keep them in good condition by watering until sold.

The Chive contains a pungent volatile oil, rich in sulphur, which is present in all the Onion tribe and causes their distinctive smell and taste, but is more delicate in this species.

It is most economical and delightful to use early in the year, especially before the spring onions come in, and also when onions are dear. It makes an excellent and more delicate substitute for flavouring, for which purpose it deserves to be more widely grown.

It is a great improvement to salads—cut fresh and chopped fine—and may be put not only in green salads, but also into cucumber salad, or sprinkled on sliced tomatoes.

Chives are also excellent in savoury omelettes, and may be chopped and boiled with potatoes that are to be mashed, or chopped fresh and sprinkled, just before serving, on the top of a dish of mashed potatoes, both as a garnish and flavouring. They may also be put into soup, either dried, or freshly cut and finely chopped, and are a welcome improvement to home-made sausages, croquettes, etc., as well as being an excellent addition to beefsteak-puddings and pies. A delicate goût is given to the dripping in which meat is fried, which is imparted to the meat itself, by adding some chopped Chives.

Finally, Chives are also useful for cutting up and mixing with the food of newly-hatched turkeys.

In *Chambers's Encyclopædia* we read:—

"This rather pretty little plant grows wild on the banks of rivers, in marshy or occasionally flooded places, and in rocky pastures in the middle latitudes of Europe and Asia, as also in the far north of North America. It is a rare native of

Britain, being only recorded with certainty from some localities in Cornwall and Northumberland. In some of the mountainous districts of Europe a variety is found, larger and stronger in all its parts, and with flowering stems more leafy. Chives are commonly cultivated in kitchen-gardens, often as an edging for plots, and are used for flavouring soups and dishes, and in salads. Their properties are very similar to those of the onion. . . . The bulbs also are by some used in preference to onions for pickling, their flavour being considered more delicate. For this purpose the clumps of bulbs are broken up in autumn or early winter, and planted in well-manured ground, in lines four or five inches apart, but standing almost close in line. In this way they become larger and more succulent by the following autumn, when they are lifted for use, the largest only being taken, and the smaller replanted for a future crop."

CLARY SAGE

(N.O. Labiatæ)

Salvia Sclarea Linn.
Local Name: Clary.

USES

As a perfume fixer; in sophisticating beer; as country wine.

The Clary Sage, a member of the order *Labiatæ,* is, like its near relative the Garden Sage, not a native of Great Britain, having first been introduced into English cultivation in the year 1562.

It is a native of Syria, Italy, Southern France, and Switzerland, but will thrive here upon almost any soil that is not too wet, though it will rot frequently upon moist ground in the winter.

The English name Clary originates in the Latin specific name *sclarea,* a word derived from *clarus,* clear. This name Clary was often popularly modified into "Clear Eye."

Clary Sage is a biennial plant, its square, brownish stems growing 2–3ft. high, hairy and with few branches. The leaves are arranged in pairs, almost stalkless and are large, almost as large as the hand, oblong and heart-shaped, wrinkled, irregularly toothed at the margins and covered with velvety hairs. The flowers are in a long, loose, terminal spike, on which they are set in whorls. The lipped corollas, similar to the Garden Sage, but smaller, are of a pale blue or white. The flowers are interspersed with large, coloured, membraneous bracts, longer than the spiny calyx. Both corollas and bracts are generally variegated with pale purple and yellowish-white. The seeds are blackish brown, "contained in long, toothed husks," as an old writer describes the calyx, and retain their germinating power for three years. The whole plant possesses a very strong, aromatic scent, somewhat resembling that of Tolu, while the taste is also aromatic, warm and slightly bitter.

CULTIVATION. Clary Sage is propagated by seed, which should be sown in spring. When fit to move, the seedlings should be transplanted to an open spot of ground, a foot apart each way, if required in large quantities. After the plants have taken root, they will require no further care but to keep them free of weeds. The winter and spring following, the leaves will be in perfection. As the plant is a biennial only, dying off in the second summer, after it has ripened seeds, there shall be young plants annually raised for use.

In August, the leaves may be gathered, and if this harvest is judiciously done, the production of foliage should continue until midsummer of the second year, when the plant will probably flower and die off, being only a biennial, so that it will be necessary to rely upon new plants for supplies of leaves.

Young plants should therefore be raised annually for use.

According to Ettmueller, this herb was first brought into use by the wine merchants of Germany, who employed it as an adulterant, infusing it with Elder flowers and then adding the liquid to the Rhenish wine, which converted it into the likeness of Muscatel. It is still called in Germany *Muskateller Salbei* (Muscatel Sage).

The leaves can be used for flavouring, either fresh or dried, in the same manner as the Garden Sage, but the plant has almost fallen into disuse as a culinary herb.

Of late there is a big trade being done with it, mainly in France, for the extraction of its oil as a perfume fixer, and there is undoubtedly a big future ahead for it for this purpose, not only on the Continent, but also in this country. The oil has a highly aromatic odour, resembling that of ambergris, and is known commercially as Clary Sage Oil or Muscatel Sage Oil.

CORIANDER

(N.O. Umbelliferæ)

Coriandrum sativum Linn.
  Local Name: Coriander.

USES

Seeds as a flavouring.

Coriander, an umbelliferous plant indigenous to southern Europe, is found occasionally in Britain in fields and waste places, and by the sides of rivers, but is rare and scarcely even naturalised, though frequently found in a semi-wild state in the East of England, having escaped from cultivation.

Coriander was originally introduced from the East, being one of the herbs brought to Britain by the Romans. As an aromatic stimulant and spice, it has been cultivated and used from very ancient times. It was employed by Hippocrates and other Greek physicians, and in the Book of Numbers, xi. 7, we read that Moses compares Manna to a Coriander seed.

The name Coriandrum, used by Pliny, is derived from *koros,* a bug, in reference to the fœtid smell of the leaves.

DESCRIPTION. It is an annual, with erect stems, 1–3ft. high, slender and branched. The lowest leaves are stalked and pinnate, the leaflets roundish or oval, slightly lobed. The segments of the uppermost leaves are linear and more divided. The flowers are in shortly-stalked umbels, 5–10 rays, pale mauve, almost white, delicately pretty. The seed clusters are very symmetrical and the seeds fall as soon as ripe. The plant is bright green, shining, glabrous and intensely fœtid.

The seeds are quite round, like tiny balls, deeply furrowed, and about the size of a Sweet Pea Seed. They retain their vitality for five or six years. On drying they lose their disagreeable scent and become fragrant—the longer they are kept the more fragrant they become, with a warm, pungent taste.

Gerarde describes it as follows: "The common kind of Coriander is a very striking herb, it has a round stalk full of branches, 2ft. long. The leaves are almost like the leaves of the parsley, but later on become more jagged, almost like the leaves of Fumitoire, but a great deal smaller and tenderer. The flowers are white and grow in round tassels like Dill."

CULTIVATION. Coriander likes a warm, dry soil, though it

does well in the somewhat heavy soil of Essex. On favourable land, the yield may reach or even exceed 1,500lbs. to the acre.

Sow in mild, dry weather in April, in shallow drills about half-inch deep and 10 or 12ins. apart, and cover in evenly with the soil. The seeds are slow in germinating. They may also be sown in March, in heat, for planting out in May. Except for keeping down the weeds, no further attention is necessary. The plants mature in about two months. As the seeds ripen, about August, the disagreeable odour gives place to a pleasant aroma, and the plants are then cut down with sickles, dried in the shade, and the fruit threshed out (see page 21). The seeds can quickly be dried on trays in the sun, or by slight artificial heat.

In the northern countries of Europe, the seeds are sometimes mixed with bread, but the chief consumption of Coriander seed in this country is in flavouring certain alcoholic liquors, for which purpose it was largely grown in Essex. Distillers of gin make use of it.

It is also much used in making little round pink or white comfits for children, and other confectionery; and, especially in the East, as an ingredient in curry-powder and other condiments. It is also a common ingredient in mixed spice.

The inhabitants of Peru are so fond of the taste and smell of this herb that it enters into almost all their dishes in such quantities as to render the odour insupportable, and the taste is objectionable to any but a native. Both in Peru and in Egypt, the leaves are put into soup.

CUMIN

(N.O. UMBELLIFERÆ)

CUMINUM CYMINUM Linn.
Local Name: Cumin.

USES

FRUITS for oil and as a condiment.

Cumin, which was in the Middle Ages one of the commonest spices of European growth, is a small annual herbaceous plant, indigenous to Upper Egypt, but from early times cultivated in Arabia (known to the Arabs as *kumoon*), India, China, and in the countries bordering on the Mediterranean.

Cumin is mentioned in Isaiah, xxviii, 25 and 27, and Matthew, xxiii, 23, and in the works of Hippocrates and Dioscorides. From Pliny we learn that the ancients took the ground seed with bread, water, or wine, and that it was accounted the best of condiments.

In the thirteenth and fourteenth centuries, when it was much in use as a culinary spice, its average price in England per lb. was 2d., equivalent to 1s. 4d. at the present day.

DESCRIPTION. Its stem is slender and branched, rarely exceeding one foot in height and somewhat angular. The leaves are divided into long, narrow segments like Fennel, but much smaller and are of a deep green colour, generally turned back at the ends. The upper leaves are nearly stalkless, but the lower ones have longer leaf-stalks. The flowers are small, rose-coloured or white, in stalked umbels with only 4–6 rays, each of which are only about one-third inch long, and bloom

in June and July, being succeeded by fruit—the so-called seeds
—which constitute the Cumin of pharmacy. They are oblong
in shape, thicker in the middle, compressed laterally about
one-fifth inch long, resembling Caraway seeds, but lighter in
colour and bristly instead of smooth and almost straight, instead of being curved. They have nine fine ridges, overlap-
ping as many oil channels, or *vittæ*. The odour and taste are
somewhat like Caraway.

After the seed has been kept for two years it begins to lose
its germinating power.

The strong, aromatic smell and warm, bitterish taste of
Cumin fruits are due to the presence of a volatile oil, which
is separated by distillation of the fruit with water.

16cwts. of the fruits yield about 44lbs. of the oil.

Cultivation. Although we get nearly all our supplies
from the Mediterranean, it would be perfectly feasible to
grow Cumin in England, as it will ripen its fruit as far
north as Norway. It is, however, rarely cultivated here, and
seeds are generally somewhat difficult to obtain.

They should be sown in small pots, filled with light soil
and plunged into a very moderate hot-bed to bring up the
plants. These should be hardened gradually in an open frame
and transplanted into a warm border of good soil, preserving
the balls of earth which adhere to the roots in the pots. Keep
clean of weeds and the plants will flower very well and will
probably perfect their seeds if the season should be warm and
favourable.

The plants are threshed when the fruit is ripe and the
"seeds" dried in the same manner as Caraway.

Cumin has now gone out of use in Europe, having been
replaced by Caraway seed, which has a more agreeable
flavour, but it is still used to a large extent in India.

Its principal employment now is as an ingredient in curry-powder, for which purpose it is imported from Bombay and Calcutta, Morocco, Sicily and Malta. It is commonly sold in Malta, where they call it *cumino aigro,* hot cumin, to distinguish it from Anise, which they term *cumino dulce,* or sweet cumin.

In France, the seeds are used for flavouring pickles, pastry and soups.

DILL

(N.O. UMBELLIFERÆ)

ANETHUM GRAVEOLENS Linn.
  Local Name: Dill.

USES

YOUNG LEAVES sometimes used for flavouring.
SEEDS in Dill vinegar.

Dill is a hardy annual, a native of the Mediterranean region and Southern Russia. It grows wild among the corn in Spain and Portugal and upon the coast of Italy, but rarely occurs as a cornfield weed in Northern Europe. In olden times it was grown in Palestine, and was well known in Pliny's time, and often mentioned by writers in the Middle Ages.

DESCRIPTION. The plant grows ordinarily from 2–2½ft. high, and is very like Fennel, though smaller, having the same feathery leaves, though seldom more than one stalk, and, unlike Fennel, its roots are only annual. It is of very upright growth, its stems smooth, shiny and hollow, and in mid-summer bearing umbels with numerous yellow flowers, whose small petals are rolled inwards. The flat fruits—the so-called "seeds"—are produced in great quantities. They are very pungent and bitter in taste, and very light, an ounce containing over 25,000 seeds. Their germinating capacity lasts for three years.

Cultivation. This annual is of very easy culture. When grown on a large scale for the sake of its fruits, it may be sown in drills 10ins. apart, in March or April, 10lbs. of the seed being drilled to the acre, and thinned out to leave 8–10ins. room each way. Sometimes the seed is sown in autumn as soon as ripe, but it is not so advisable as spring sowing. Careful attention must be given to the destruction of weeds. Mowing is begun as the lower seeds begin to fall, the others ripening on the straw. In dry periods, cutting is best done in early morning, or late evening, care being taken to handle with the least possible shaking to prevent loss. The loose sheaves are built into stacks of about 20 sheaves, tied together. In hot weather, threshing may be done in the field, spreading the sheaves on a large canvas sheet and beating out. The crop is considered somewhat exhaustive of soil fertility. The average yield is about 7cwt. of Dill fruits per acre.

The seeds are finally dried by spreading out on trays in the sun, or for a short time over the moderate heat of a stove, shaking occasionally.

The taste of the seeds is an odd blend of different flavours, resembling Caraway, but distinct. The seeds are smaller, flatter and lighter than Caraway, and have a pleasant aromatic odour. They contain about 3–4 per cent. of a volatile oil, obtained by distillation, upon which the medicinal action of the fruit depends.

As a sweet herb, Dill is not much used in this country. When employed, it is for flavouring soups, sauces, etc., for which purpose the young leaves only are required. The leaves added to fish, or mixed with pickled cucumbers are said to give them a spicy taste.

Dill vinegar, however, forms a popular household condiment. It is made by soaking the seeds in good vinegar for a few days before using.

The French use Dill seeds for flavouring preserves, cakes and pastry, as well as for flavouring sauces, but their use of them does not appeal to us in this country.

Perhaps the chief culinary use of Dill seeds is in pickling cucumbers: they are employed in this way chiefly in Germany, where pickled cucumbers are largely eaten.

Like the other umbelliferous fruits and volatile oils both Dill fruit and Oil of Dill possess stimulant, aromatic, carminative and stomachic properties. Dill Oil is very similar in composition to Caraway Oil.

SOME OLD-FASHIONED DILL RECIPES

Dill and Collyflower Pickle.—Boil the Collyflowers till they fall in pieces; then with some of the stalk and worst of the flower boil it in a part of the liquer till pretty strong. Then being taken off strain it; and when settled, clean it from the bottom. Then with Dill, gross pepper, a pretty quantity of salt, when cold add as much vinegar as will make it sharp and pour all upon the Collyflower.

From *Acetaria,* a book about Sallets, 1680, by John Evelyn.

To Pickle Cucumbers in Dill.—Gather the tops of the ripest dill and cover the bottom of the vessel, and lay a layer of Cucumbers and another of Dill till you have filled the vessel within a handful of the top. Then take as much water as you think will fill the vessel and mix it with salt and a quarter of a pound of allom to a gallon of water and poure it on them and press them down with a stone on them and keep them covered close. For that use I think the water will be best boyl'd and cold, which will keep longer sweet, or if you like not this pickle, doe it with water, salt and white wine vinegar, or (if you please) pour the water and salt on them scalding hot which will make them ready to use the sooner.

From *Receipt Book* of Joseph Cooper, Cook to Charles I, 1640.

FENNEL

(N.O. Umbelliferæ)

Fœniculum vulgare Miller.
    Local Name: Common Fennel.
Fœniculum dulce Miller.
    Local Name: Sweet Fennel.

USES

Leaves blanched for salads; as potherb and for garnishing.

Fennel, a hardy perennial, umbelliferous herb, with yellow flowers and feathery leaves, grows wild in most parts of temperate Europe, apparently indigenous to the shores of the Mediterranean, eastwards, but is largely cultivated in the South of France, Saxony, Galicia and Russia, as well as in India and Persia. It is now naturalised in some parts of this country, especially in Devon and Cornwall and on chalk cliffs near the sea.

The plant was cultivated by the ancient Romans for its aromatic fruits and succulent, edible shoots. Its culture was ordered by Charlemagne upon the imperial farms, and it is frequently mentioned in Anglo-Saxon cookery prior to the Norman Conquest. At the present day, it is most popular in Italy and France.

The whole plant has a warm, aromatic taste and was highly esteemed by the ancient Greeks, who had a theory that serpents had recourse to it to cure blindness. It was also supposed to confer longevity, strength and courage, and Longfellow has written a poem about it to this effect. William Coles, in *Nature's Paradise*, 1650, said that "both the seeds, leaves and roots of our Garden Fennel are much used in drinks and broths for those that are grown fat, to abate their unwieldiness and cause them to grow more gaunt and lank."

DESCRIPTION. Its stout stems, 4 to 5ft. high, erect and cylindrical, bright green and so smooth as to seem polished, are much branched. The bright golden flowers are produced in July and August.

Fennel is naturally a very ornamental graceful plant, but in the kitchen-garden, the stems are generally cut down to secure a constant crop of green leaves for flavouring and garnishing, so that the plant is seldom seen in the same perfection as in the wild state. In the original wild condition, it is variable as to size, habit, shape and colour of the leaf, number of rays in the flower-head or umbel, and shape of fruit, but it has been under cultivation for so long that there are now several well-marked species. The Common Garden Fennel (*F. capillaceum* or *officinale*) is distinguished from the wild form (*F. vulgare*) by having much stouter, taller, tubular and larger stems, and less divided leaves, but the chief distinction is that the leaf stalks form a curved sheath around the stem, often even as far up as the base of the leaf above.

The flower stalks or pedicels of the umbels are also sturdier, and the seeds, ¼ to ½in. long, are double the size of the wild ones.

CULTIVATION. Fennel will thrive anywhere, and a plantation will last for years. It is easily propagated by seeds, sown early in April in ordinary soil. It likes plenty of sun and is adapted to dry and sunny situations, not needing heavily manured ground, though it will probably yield more on rich soil, on the stiff side. From 4½ to 5lb. of seed are sown per acre, either in drills, 15ins. apart, lightly, just covered with soil, and the plants afterwards thinned to a similar distance, or thinly in a bed and transplanted when large enough. The fruit is heavy, and a crop of 15cwt. per acre would probably be obtained. Cutting should be done in the end of September, as the lower fruits begin to fall, the others ripening on the straw. In dry periods, cutting is best done in early morning or late evening. The loose sheaves are built into small stacks of about twenty sheaves tied together, and the fruits separated by threshing in the same manner as Dill.

They can be dried either on trays in the sun or by gentle heat over a stove, shaking occasionally.

The cessation of the supply of Fennel fruits from the Continent during the war led to its being grown more extensively here, any crop produced being almost certain to sell well.

The fruits of the cultivated plants, especially those grown in Saxony, are alone official, as they yield the most volatile oil. Fennel fruits occur in several commercial varieties, varying in colour, size and appearance. Saxon fruits are greenish or yellowish-brown in colour, oblong, smaller and straighter than the French or Sweet Fennel (*Fœniculum dulce*), which is the cultivated form of the Wild Fennel, *Fœniculum vulgare,* and is distinguished by its greater length, more oblong form and sweet taste; its anise-like odour is also stronger, but it yields only about 2 per cent. of oil. The chief commercial varieties, Saxon, Galician and Russian, all yield 4 to 5 per cent. of volatile oil.

For family use, ½oz. of seed will produce an ample supply of plants, and for several years, either from the established roots or by re-seeding. Unless seed is needed for household or sowing purposes, the flower stems should be cut as soon as they appear.

It was formerly the practice to boil Fennel with all fish, and it was mainly cultivated in kitchen-gardens for this purpose. Its leaves are served nowadays with salmon to correct the oily indigestibility thereof, and are also put into sauce, in the same way as parsley, to be eaten with boiled mackerel. The seeds are also used for flavouring, and a carminative oil is distilled from them, with a sweetish aromatic odour and flavour, which is employed in the making of cordials and liqueurs.

It is one of the plants which is said to be disliked by flies, and powdered Fennel has the effect of driving away flies from kennels and stables.

In Italy and France, the tender leaves are often used for garnishes and to add flavour to salads, and are also added finely chopped, to sauces served with puddings.

The tender stems are employed in soups in Italy, though more frequently eaten raw as a salad. The famous "Cartucci," of Naples, consists of the peeled stems, cut when the plant is about to bloom, and served with a dressing of vinegar and pepper. In olden days, poor people used to eat Fennel to satisfy the cravings of hunger on fast days.

FINNCHIO, or FLORENCE FENNEL (*Fœniculum azoricum*), is a variety grown in Italy, a small annual, even when full-grown and producing seed rarely exceeding 2ft. in height.

It is a very thick-set plant, the stem joints are very close together and their bases much swollen. The large, finely-cut leaves are borne on very broad, pale green, or almost whitish stalks, which overlap at their bases somewhat like celery, swelling at maturity to form a sort of head or irregular ball —often as big as a man's head and resembling a tuber.

CULTIVATION. The cultivation is much the same as for Common Fennel, though it requires richer soil, and owing to the dwarf nature of the plant the rows and the plants may be placed closer together, the seedlings only 6 to 8ins. apart. They are very thirsty, and require watering frequently in dry weather. When the "tubers" swell and attain the size of an egg, draw the soil slightly around it, half covering it; cutting may begin about ten days later. The flower-heads should be removed as they appear.

Florence Fennel should be cooked in vegetarian or meat stock, and served with either a rich butter sauce or cream dressing. It suggests celery in flavour, but is sweeter, and very pleasantly fragrant. In ordinary times it can be bought of Italian greengrocers in London. In Italy it is one of the commonest and most popular of vegetables.

FENNEL SAUCE

Have boiling salt and water ready, take a bunch of Fennel and let it boil for two or three minutes; take it out and squeeze out as much of the water as possible, then chop the Fennel very fine, but *not* the stalks. Take a tablespoonful of baked flour and knead into it three ounces of butter, then stir into half a pint of boiling water. Boil for ten minutes and then stir in the chopped Fennel.

A few recipes culled from Cookery books of by-gone times may prove of interest.

A Sallet of Fennel.—Take young Fennel, about a span

77

long in the spring, tye it up in bunches as you do Sparragrass; when your Skillet boyle, put in enough to make a dish; when it is boyled and drained, dish it up as you do Sparragrass, pour on butter and vinegar and send it up.

From *The Whole Body of Cookery Dissected*, 1675, by William Rabisha.

Fennel and Gooseberry Sauce.—Brown some butter in a saucepan with a pinch of flour, then put in a few chives shred small, add a little Irish broth to moisten it, season with salt and pepper; make these boil, then put in two or three sprigs of Fennel and some Gooseberries. Let all simmer together till the Gooseberries are soft and then put in some Cullis.

From *Receipt Book* of Henry Howard, Cook to the Duke of Ormond, 1710.

HOREHOUND

(N.O. LABIATÆ)

MARRUBIUM VULGARE Linn.
Local Name: Horehound.

USES

DRIED LEAVES as Tea; also used to make Horehound Ale.

White Horehound is a perennial herbaceous plant, found all over Europe and indigenous to Britain. Like many other plants of the *Labiatæ* tribe, it flourishes in waste places and by roadsides, particularly in the counties of Norfolk and Suffolk, where it is also cultivated in the corners of cottage gardens for making tea and candy.

It was formerly widely esteemed in cookery as well as medicine, but its flavour is too strong and lasting to be appreciated as a seasoning in modern cookery—the generic name is, indeed, derived from the Hebrew *Marrob,* "a bitter juice," and it is considered to have been one of the bitter herbs which the Jews were ordered to take for the Feast of Passover.

DESCRIPTION. The plant is bushy, producing numerous annual, quadrangular and branching stems, a foot or more in height, on which the whitish flowers are borne in crowded, axillary, woolly whorls. The leaves are much wrinkled, opposite, petiolate, about one inch long, covered with white, felted hairs, which give them a woolly appearance, from which the common name Horehound (Hoarhound) is derived. They have a curious, musky smell, which is diminished by drying, and lost on keeping. Horehound flowers from June to September.

CULTIVATION. White Horehound is a hardy plant, easily grown, which flourishes best in a dry, poor soil. It can be propagated from seeds sown in spring, cuttings, or by dividing the roots, the most usual method. If raised from seed, the seedlings should be planted out in the spring, in rows, with a space of about 9ins. or more between each plant. No further culture will be needed save keeping clean from weeds. It does not blossom until it is two years old. Often the clumps may be divided, or layers or cuttings may be used for propagation. No protection need be given as the plants are hardy. It is much cultivated in Southern France, and it might probably pay to cultivate it more in this country.

Horehound Tea may be made by pouring boiling water on the fresh or dried leaves, one ounce of the latter to the pint, and sweetening this with honey. A wineglassful may be taken three or four times a day.

Candied Horehound is best made from the fresh plant by boiling it down until the juice is extracted, then adding sugar at the rate of 8 or 10lbs. to one pint of the strong decoction. This is boiled till of a very thick consistency and poured into moulds, or small paper cases, previously well dusted with finely-powdered white sugar, or poured on dusted marble slabs, and cut into squares when cool.

Bees are very fond of Horehound nectar, and the honey they make from the flowers where they are abundant has a high reputation, and used to be almost as popular as Horehound candy.

The herb is also brewed and made into Horehound Ale, an appetising and healthful beverage, much drunk in Norfolk and other country districts. (See Part II.)

HYSSOP

(N.O. LABIATÆ)

HYSSOPUS OFFICINALIS Linn.
  Local Name: Hyssop.

USES

LEAVES used to make oil for perfumery and liqueur-flavouring; leaves occasionally used in salads.

The Hyssop is a perennial evergreen under-shrub, belonging to the order *Labiatæ* and is a native of the Mediterranean region.

It gets its name from the Greek. The *Hyssopos* of Dioscorides was named *Azob,* a holy herb, because used for cleaning sacred places. Hence it is alluded to in this sense scripturally: "Purge me with Hyssop, and I shall be clean." But though well known in ancient times, this plant is probably not the Hyssop used to sprinkle blood by the Jewish priests, which is now considered to be a species of Marjoram (*Origanum Maru*), which smells of and apparently contains the modern antiseptic Thymol.

In ancient and mediæval times Hyssop was grown for its medicinal qualities, for ornament and for cookery. It is now chiefly cultivated only as an ornamental plant.

J. T. Burgess, in *English Wild Flowers,* says:—

"The change in the calendar has turned the pretty Milkwort (*Polygala vulgaris*), the Rogation or procession flower of our ancestors, like many old spring flowers, into a summer flower, for it is seldom now in bloom until June. It grows but a few inches high, but its racemes of reddish flowers, varying sometimes into purple and blue, are well known to the wanderers in healthy pastures. In Gerarde's time this plant was known as hedge hyssop, and sold as such. This little plant was used in garlands to decorate the windows during procession week."

DESCRIPTION. Hyssop is a bushy herb, growing from 1ft. to 1½ and sometimes 2ft. high, with quadrangular stems, and narrow, entire leaves placed on them opposite to one another in pairs. The flowers are in small clusters, crowded in terminal, one-sided spikes. There are three varieties, known respectively by their blue, red and white flowers, which are in bloom from June to October, and are often employed as edging plants. Grown with Catmint it makes a lovely border, backed with Lavender and Rosemary. The leaves, stems and flowers possess a highly aromatic odour, and a hot, bitter flavour.

Cultivation. Hyssop may be propagated by seeds, sown in April, or by dividing the plants in spring and autumn, or by cuttings, made in spring and inserted in a shady situation. Plants raised from seeds or cuttings, should, when large enough, be planted out about 1ft. apart each way, and kept watered till established. They succeed best in a warm aspect and in a light, rather dry soil. The plants require cutting down occasionally, but do not need much further attention, being perfectly hardy.

Distillers extract a colourless oil from the leaves, which is used in perfumery and for flavouring liqueurs. If required for this purpose the shoots should be cut when the flowers first open. From 400 to 500lbs. of the fresh plant yield 1lb. of oil.

As a kitchen herb Hyssop has greatly gone out of use, because it is too strongly flavoured. It was formerly employed in broths, and its tender leaves and shoots are still occasionally added to salads, more in the nature of a condiment, to supply a bitter taste.

LOVAGE

(N.O. Umbelliferæ)

Levisticum officinale Koch.
Local name: Lovage.

USES

Young Stems, treated like Angelica for flavouring and confectionery.

This umbelliferous plant is a perennial, a native of the Mediterranean. The large, dark green, shining, radical leaves are usually divided into two or three segments. The thick, hollow, erect stems divide towards the top to form opposite, whorled branches, which bear umbels of yellow flowers, followed by extremely aromatic, hollowed fruits, with three prominent ribs.

CULTIVATION. Propagation is by division of roots or by seeds. Rich moist soil is required. In late summer, when the seed ripens, it is sown, and the seedlings transplanted either in the autumn or as early in spring as possible to their permanent places. Root division is performed in early spring. The plants should last for several years if the ground is kept well cultivated.

Formerly Lovage was used for a great variety of purposes, but now it is restricted almost wholly to confectionery, the young stems being treated like those of Angelica.

The leaf-stalks and stem bases were formerly blanched like celery.

MARIGOLD

(N.O. COMPOSITÆ)

CALENDULA OFFICINALIS Linn.
Local name: Pot Marigold.

USES

LEAVES can be eaten as salad.
FLOWERS used as colouring.

The Pot Marigold is familiar to everyone, with its pale-green leaves and golden and orange flowers. It is an annual herb of the natural order *Compositæ,* a native of southern Europe, but perfectly hardy in this country. Its Latin name, suggestive of its flowering habit, signifies "blooming through the months." It is a general favourite, especially in country gardens, easily grown and so free a bloomer that it continues in blossom from early summer until the first hard frosts arrive and kill the plants.

CULTIVATION. For the garden, the seed is usually started in a hotbed during March or April, and the plants pricked out in shallow boxes, 2ins. apart, and hardened off in the usual way. When the weather becomes settled, they are set a foot or 15ins. apart in rather poor soil, preferably light and sandy, with sunny exposure. The seed may also be sown in the open, and the seedlings transplanted when about 2ins. high. When once established, the plants will increase from year to year, if allowed to seed themselves; the seeds ripen in August and September, and if permitted to scatter, will furnish a supply of young plants in the spring.

Marigolds were well-known to Herbalists of old time as garden flowers, as well as for other uses, such as in cookery. It was cultivated in the kitchen garden and the flowers, after being dried, were boiled in broth, an old superstition being that they raised the spirits and cheered the heart.

Only the ray florets are to be used and they must be dried quickly, out of the sun and in a current of warm air. They must be placed loosely on large sheets of paper, care being taken that they should not touch each other or they will become discoloured.

A yellow dye has been made from the flowers, and marigolds have also been used as a substitute for Saffron for colouring butter and cheese, and also employed for colouring Pot Pourri. The single marigold is supposed to be better for a potherb than the double.

MARIGOLD BUNS

Dry one pound of flour, and work into it 3oz. of lard and the same weight of butter. When well mixed with the flour stir in a teaspoonful of baking powder, ¼lb. of sugar, and a tiny pinch of salt.

Saffron buns can be made without fruit, but they are much better with fruit. Wash and dry a handful of sultanas and cut up some candied peel into small chunks and throw into the mixing bowl. Put some dried marigold petals into a small muslin bag and set to soak in a small cup of very hot milk. While the milk is cooling an egg should be well beaten. Remove the marigold petals from the milk and add the beaten egg to it.

Then stir the mixture into the bowl containing the dry ingredients, and the whole should be beaten for some minutes—the longer the better. The mixture should then be put into bun tins and baked in a moderate oven.

DRIED MARIGOLD PETALS

Many women in the country still dry marigolds for culinary purposes. This is done as follows: when the flowers seem quite dry rub the petals from the flowers and bottle for use. When making a stew or soup of any kind, just a pinch of the marigold petals will give it a very pleasant flavour.

MARJORAM

(N.O. LABIATÆ)

ORIGANUM VULGARE Linn.
   Local Name: Wild Marjoram.
ORIGANUM ONITES Linn.
   Local Name: Perennial Marjoram.
ORIGANUM MARJORANA Linn.
   Local Name: Sweet Marjoram; Knotted Marjoram.
ORIGANUM HERACLEOTICUM Linn.
   Local Name: Winter Marjoram.

USES

LEAVES for flavouring and other culinary purposes; excellent in salads.
OIL for perfuming toilet articles and soap.
FLOWER TOPS yield a dye; also used to put in table beer and flavour Saxon ale.

There are two species of Marjoram generally cultivated for culinary use, Pot or Perennial Marjoram (*Origanum Onites*) of southern Europe, and Sweet or Knotted Marjoram (*Origanum Marjorana*) native to North Africa, which is also perennial in its native habitat, but because of its liability to be killed by frost when grown in our cooler climate, is treated as an annual and grown only from seed. Both are largely used for seasonings, and our British Marjoram (*Origanum vulgare*) is also aromatic and has likewise been used for culinary purposes, though it is more especially used for medicinal purposes—in herbal medicine—for which the cultivated species are rarely employed in this country.

A third species is sometimes cultivated for culinary use, Winter Marjoram (*Origanum Heracleoticum*) a native of Greece, but hardy enough to thrive in England in a dry soil.

The generic name, *Origanum,* is derived from two Greek words, meaning delight of the mountain, some of the species being found commonly upon mountain sides. The perennial species, *O. Onites,* is the one longest associated with civilisation, mentioned by Pliny, and the great Herbalists of the Middle Ages and the sixteenth century. The Sweet Marjoram *O. Marjorana,* is considered to be the species regarded in India as sacred to Vishnu and Siva.

Description. Pot Marjoram, *O. Onites,* is a hardy perennial, growing nearly 2ft. high, in branched clumps, the stems woody and often purplish, bearing numerous short-stalked, oval leaves about an inch long, nearly entire, and hairy beneath, and terminal clusters of short spikes of little pale-lilac or purplish blossoms with reddish bracts, blooming from the end of June through August. The oval, brown seeds are very minute. There is a variety with white flowers and light green stalks, and another with variegated leaves used for ornamental purposes.

Sweet or Knotted Marjoram, *O. Marjorana,* is much more erect and more bush-like, has smaller, narrower leaves, whiter flowers, green bracts, and larger seeds. It begins to flower in the end of June or early July, and obtains its name of "Knotted" Marjoram from the flowers being collected into round, close heads like knots.

Wild Marjoram, *O. vulgare,* a perennial herb with creeping roots, sends up woody stems about a foot high, branched above, and frequently purple in colour; it grows freely in England, being particularly abundant in calcareous soils, as in the South Eastern counties. The leaves are broader, and the flower spikes looser and fuller than the cultivated varieties.

In all the species the whole plant has a strong, peculiar, fragrant, balsamic odour, and a warm, bitterish aromatic taste, both of which properties are preserved when the herb is dried.

CULTIVATION. All the Marjorams do best in a warm situation, and dry light soil.

Pot Marjoram, when once established, may readily be propagated by cuttings taken in early summer, inserted under a hand-glass, and later planted out with a space of 1ft. between the rows and nearly as much from plant to plant, as it likes plenty of room. It may also be increased by division of roots in April, or by slipping pieces off the plants with roots to them and planting with trowel or dibber, taking care to water well. In May, they grow quickly after the operation. It is also very easy to grow from seed. Sow moderately thin, in dry, mild weather in March, in shallow drills, about ½in. deep and 8 or 9ins. apart, covered in evenly with the soil. Transplant afterwards, when a few inches tall, to about a foot apart each way. The seeds are very slow in germinating. From the very start, the plants must be kept free from weeds and the soil loose and open. The plants will last for years.

Sweet or Knotted Marjoram, as already stated, is not really an annual, but is usually treated as such, as the plants will not stand the winter outside, so must be sown every year. Seeds may be sown for an early supply in March on a gentle hot-bed, and again, in a warm position, in light soil, in the open ground during April. Plants do well if sown in April, though long in germinating. The seed is small and should be sown either in drills, 9ins. apart, or broadcast, on the surface, trodden, raked evenly and watered in dry weather. On account of the slowness of germination, care should be taken that the seedlings are not choked with weeds which, being of much quicker growth, are likely to harm them if not destroyed. Weeds should be removed by hand, until the plants are large enough for the small hoe to be used. Seed may also be sown in May. In common with other aromatic herbs, such as Fennel, Basil, Dill, etc., it is not subject to the attacks of birds, as many other seeds are. When about 1in. high, thin out to 6 or 8ins. apart each way. It begins to flower in the end of June, when the first cutting of the herb may be taken.

Winter Marjoram, *O. heracleoticum,* is generally propagated by division of the roots in autumn.

When it is desired to dry the leaves for winter use the stems should be cut just as the flowers begin to appear, and dried in the usual manner. If seed is wanted, cut the stems soon after the flowers fall, when the scales around the seeds look as if they are beginning to dry. Dry the cut stems on trays of some closely-woven material to prevent loss of seed. When the stems are thoroughly dry they must be threshed and rubbed before being placed in sieves, first of coarse, then of fine, mesh.

The Marjorams are some of the most familiar of our kitchen herbs, and are cultivated for the use of their aromatic leaves, either in a green or dried state, for flavouring and other culinary purposes, being mainly put into stuffings. Sweet Marjoram leaves are also excellent in salads. The tops are also sometimes put into table beer, to give it an aromatic flavour and make it keep, and before the introduction of hops, they were nearly as much in demand for ale brewing as the ground ivy or wood sage. It is said that Marjoram or Wild Thyme, laid by milk in a dairy will prevent it being turned by thunder.

It was once greatly popular for herb tea, drunk in cases of headache and asthma, and large quantities of it are still gathered and hung up to dry in cottages in Kent and other counties for making Marjoram tea.

Among herbs Marjoram excels in flavour and is not used frequently enough in the modern kitchen. It can be used with advantage in stuffing and also to flavour soups. Marjoram leaves, dried and powdered, and sprinkled over a joint of roast pork is a welcome addition. In small quantities it forms a good flavouring with white fish.

HERB POWDER

Take fresh Marjoram, basil, bay-leaf, thyme, parsley, and dry in the sun until brittle, pick carefully off the stalk, and rub the leaves into a fine powder. Add a small quantity of dried and pounded lemon peel, allowing one saltspoonful of salt and half a saltspoonful of pepper to each ounce of the powdered herbs. Take a piece of coarse muslin and sift the powdered mixture, then put in dry bottles and cork firmly. This powder is excellent for flavouring purposes.

MINT

(N.O. LABIATÆ)

MENTHA SPICATA Linn.
    Local Name: Spearmint.
MENTHA PIPERITA Linn.
    Local Name: Peppermint.
MENTHA PULEGIUM Linn.
    Local Name: Pennyroyal.

Leaves for culinary purposes.
Herb used for distillation of oil.

There are three chief species of Mint in general use: Spearmint, *Mentha Spicata;* Peppermint, *Mentha piperita;* and Pennyroyal, *Mentha Pulegium,* the first being the one ordinarily used for cooking, and the others being valuable medicinal herbs, whose virtues we need not consider here. Spearmint has also medicinal uses though not now recognised by The British Pharmacopœia, but it is with its familiar culinary uses that we are now concerned.

This common Garden Mint, also known as Mackerel Mint and Lamb Mint, is not a native of these islands, though growing so freely in every garden, but is originally a native of the Mediterranean region, and was introduced into Britain by the Romans, being largely cultivated by them and by other Mediterranean nations. It was in great request by the Romans, and Pliny mentions that they made a practice of using it in their cookery. Gerarde renders what he says of it as: "The smell of mint does stir up the minde and the taste to a greedy desire of meate." Ovid represents the hospitable Baucis and Philemon as scouring their board with green mint before laying upon it the food intended for their divine guests. The ancients had a notion that mint would prevent the coagulation of milk and its acid fermentation. Gerarde, quoting Pliny, says: "It will not suffer milk to curdle in the stomach, and therefore it is put in milk that is drunke." Pliny also recommends a Crown of Mint to be worn when studying, as it "exhilarates the mind and is therefore proper for students."

Many other references are made to it in old writings, among them that of the payment by the Pharisees of tithes of Mint, Anise and Cumin, prove that the herb has been highly esteemed for many centuries.

Its generic name, *Mentha,* is derived from the mythological origin ascribed to it. Minthe (we learn from Ovid) was a nymph, who because of the love Pluto bore her, was from motives of jealousy metamorphosed by Proserpine into the plant we now call Mint.

DESCRIPTION. From creeping rootstocks, erect, square stems rise to a height of about 2ft., having very short stalked acute-pointed, lance-shaped, wrinkled, bright green leaves with finely toothed edges, and smooth surfaces. The small flowers are densely arranged in cylindrical, slender, tapering spikes, are pinkish or lilac in colour, have two-lipped corollas, and are followed by very few roundish, minute, brown seeds.

CULTIVATION. A moist situation is preferable, but mint will succeed in almost any soil, when once started into growth, and does best in a partially-shaded position. If in a sheltered spot it will start earlier in the spring than if exposed. Where a long or regular supply is required, it is a good plan to have at least one bed in a sunny and sheltered, and another in a shady position, when gatherings may be made both early and late.

As the plant is a perennial, spreading by means of its underground, creeping stems, propagation may easily be effected by lifting the roots in February or March, dividing them—every piece showing a joint will grow—and planting again, in shallow trenches, covering with 2ins. of soil, 6ft. apart in rows and 8ins. between the rows are the right distances to allow.

Cuttings in summer or offsets in spring may also be utilised for increasing stock. Cuttings may be taken at almost any time during the summer, always choosing the young shoots, these being struck on a shady border of light soil and kept moist; or a better plan, if possible, is to insert them in a frame, keeping them close and moist till rooted. Cuttings or young shoots will also strike freely in good size boxes in a heated greenhouse in the early spring, and after the tops have been taken off two or three times for use, the plants may be hardened off and planted outside.

The beds are much benefited by an annual top-dressing of rich soil, applied towards the close of autumn, when all remaining stalks should be cut down to the ground. A liberal top-dressing of short, decayed manure, such as that from an old hot-bed or mushroom bed, annually, either in the spring, when it commences to grow, or better still, perhaps, after the first or second cutting, will ensure luxuriant growth. Frequent cuttings of shoots constitute a great drain on the plants, and if not properly nourished they will fail, more or less. To have really good Mint, the plantation should be re-made about every three years.

When the plants are about to bloom, the stalks should be cut on a dry day and dried for culinary use in the winter, being suspended in bunches to dry, in the usual manner.

If the herb is to be distilled for the sake of its volatile oil, it should be taken to the distillery as soon as possible after picking.

A good stock should be kept up, so that plenty may be available for FORCING. For culinary purposes green leaves are always preferable to dry ones, and forcing is very easy, the only preparation being the insertion of a quantity of good roots in a box of light soil, which should be placed in a temperature of about 60° F. and watered freely as soon as growth starts. Cuttings may be made in two or three weeks. Forcing will generally be necessary from November to May—a succession being kept up by the introduction at intervals of an additional supply of roots. Often Mint is so grown both upon and under the benches in greenhouses, and the demand for the young tender stems and leaves during the winter is sufficient to make the plants pay well.

MINT DISEASE. Unfortunately, Mint is susceptible to a disease which in some gardens has completely destroyed it. This disease, which from its characteristic symptoms is known as Rust, is incurable. The fungus which causes it develops inside the plant, and therefore cannot be reached by any fungicide, and as it is perennial, living in the underground stems when the shoots are dead, it cannot be got rid of by cutting off the latter. All that can be done is to prevent the spread of the disease by digging up all plants that show any sign of Rust. The same ground should not be used again for Mint for several years. Healthy stock should be obtained and planted in uninfected soil some distance away. On account of this liability of Mint to Rust, it is advisable not to have it all in one bed.

There are several forms of Garden Mint, the true variety being of bolt, upright growth, with fairly large and broad leaves, pointed and sharply serrated at the edges, and of a rich, bright green colour. Another variety is much smaller and less erect in growth, with darker leaves, but it possesses the same odour and flavour; and another has comparatively large, broad or rounded leaves, clothed with soft hairs, but this, though distinct from what is known as "horse mint," is inferior to the true "spear" variety. A form with its leaves slightly crisped is common in gardens under the name of *Mentha crispa*.

Mint has been estimated to yield from four to five tons per acre, from which 15 to 20 cwt. of dry should be obtained.

Average yields per acre are, however, taken when crops are at maturity, and an estimate of the first cutting crop is hard to form, and is likely to be less profitable than succeeding years on account of initial expenses.

When eaten with lamb in the form of Mint Sauce, it greatly aids the digestion, as it makes the crude, albuminous fibres of the immature meat more digestible. The oil stimulates the digestive system, and prevents septic changes within the intestines.

Mint Jelly can be used instead of Mint Sauce, in the same manner as Red Currant Jelly is eaten with Mutton and Hare. It may be made by steeping the Mint leaves in apple jelly, or in one of the various kinds of commercial pectin jellies. The jelly should be a delicate shade of green. A handful of leaves should colour and flavour about ½ pt. of jelly. Strain the liquid through a jelly bag to remove all particles of Mint before allowing to set.

The fresh sprigs of Mint are used to flavour green peas and also new potatoes, being boiled with them, and the powdered, dried leaves are used with pea soup and also in seasonings.

In the fourteenth century, Mint, we find, was used for whitening the teeth, and its distilled oil is still used to flavour toothpastes, etc., and in America, especially, to flavour chewing gums.

It has been said that mice are so averse to the smell of Mint, either fresh or dried, that they will leave untouched any food where it is scattered, and not go near a larder if it is present.

MINT AND CREAM CHEESE SANDWICHES

Season a cream cheese with salt, a touch of paprika, and

finely-minced mint—a tablespoonful of mint to 3ozs. of cheese. Should the cream cheese be too hard to spread easily on the bread and butter, beat it up with a little fresh cream.

MINT CHUTNEY

Chop up ½lb. tomatoes, 1lb. apples, three large pepper-corns, six small onions, and a breakfast-cup of mint leaves. Take three breakfast-cups of vinegar and bring to scalding point; add to it two breakfast-cups of brown sugar, two tea-spoonfuls of dry mustard, one and a half cups of seeded raisins, two teaspoonfuls of salt, and one red pepper pod. Then mix in the chopped tomatoes, etc. Have some jars standing ready in boiling water. Use them one by one, taking each as required out of the boiling water and filling it at once with the chutney, and cover air-tight, but do not otherwise heat the chutney. It will keep perfectly and im-prove with age. Do not use it for a month after it is made.

MINT VINEGAR

Take some fresh mint leaves, bruise them, and put into a glass jar so as to fill it loosely. Fill the jar up with vinegar. Cover it and let it stand in a cool place for 14 days, then pour off the vinegar through a strainer, and bottle. This will be found an excellent substitute for tarragon vinegar in any recipes where this is to be added, and also gives a pleasant flavour to salad dressings.

MINT AND PEAS

Put some fresh green peas in a pan with a lump of butter, salt and pepper to taste, placing at the side of the fire to cook gently until done. Then stir in about two tablespoonfuls of minced mint to each quart of peas, and a small teaspoonful of sugar.

THREE WAYS OF MAKING MINT SAUCE

(A)

Take a cupful of well-chopped mint, moisten it thoroughly with boiling water, cover closely, and let it stand until cold. When cold stir in an equal quantity of orange marmalade.

(B)

Take a cupful of vinegar, add a pinch of salt, then heat until it is just below boiling point; take an equal quantity of finely-chopped mint and pour the hot vinegar over it. Let it steep for quite ten minutes, and then stir in three tablespoonfuls of heather honey. Should this be unobtainable, use soft brown sugar.

(c)

Take a good cupful of red currant jelly and mix into it two tablespoonfuls of finely-chopped mint. This is a much better way than serving the red currant jelly and mint sauce separately with roast lamb.

ICED MINT PUNCH

Mix dry tea with about three times the bulk of finely-chopped mint and then infuse in the ordinary way. Strain through a sieve and in each 1½pts. of liquid add the juice from a small tin of pineapple. Rub down three or four lumps of sugar on a lemon into the mixture, and add the juice of two lemons. Set on ice to cool and serve in glasses with a lump of ice, a straw, and a sprig of mint.

ANOTHER METHOD

Mix dry coffee with twice the quantity of fine-chopped mint, infuse in the usual way, and make in the same way as the previous recipe for tea.

A THIRD RECIPE

Infuse minted tea or coffee as in the two previous recipes, then dissolve about a teacupful of red currant jelly in one pint of boiling water. When the two jugs of liquid are quite cold, mix them, adding the juice of two oranges and sugar to taste. Cool on ice and serve as before with a sprig of mint.

PARSLEY

(N.O. Umbelliferæ)

Carum Petroselinum Benth. & Hook.f.
Local Name: Parsley.

USES

Leaves for culinary purposes.
Fruits to produce an oil.

The Garden Parsley, a member of the order *Umbelliferæ,* is not indigenous to Britain: Linnæus stated its wild habitat to be Sardinia, whence it was brought to England and apparently first cultivated here in 1548. Bentham and De Candolle considered it a native of the Eastern Mediterranean regions.

Petroselinum, the specific name of the Parsley, from which our English name is derived, is of classic origin, and is said to have been assigned to it by Dioscorides. It is derived from the habitat of the plant, which naturally grows among rocks, the Greek word for which is *Petros.*

This name in the Middle Ages became corrupted into *Petrocilium*—this was anglicised into Petersylinge, Persele, Persely, and finally Parsley.

Many of the ancient writings contain references to it, and some give directions for its cultivation.

The Greeks held Parsley in high esteem, crowning the victors with chaplets of Parsley at the Isthmian games, and making with it wreaths for adorning the tombs of their dead. The herb was never brought to table of old, being held sacred to oblivion and to the dead. It was reputed to have sprung from the blood of a Greek hero, Archemorus, the forerunner of death, and Homer relates that chariot horses were fed by warriors with the leaves. Greek gardens were often bordered with Parsley and Rue. It is undoubtedly the most widely-grown of all garden herbs.

Several cultivated varieties exist, the principal being the common plain-leaved, the curled-leaved, the Hamburg or broad-leaved and the celery-leaved. Of the variety *crispum*, or curled-leaved, there are no less than 37 forms; the most valuable are those of a compact habit with close, perfectly curled leaves. The common sort bears close leaves, but it is of somewhat hardier nature than those of which the leaves are curled; the latter are, however, superior in every way. The variety *crispum* was grown in very early days, being even mentioned by Pliny.

The Hamburg, or turnip-rooted Parsley is grown only for the sake of its enlarged flesh tap-root. No mention appears to have been made by the ancients, or in the Middle Ages, of this variety, which Miller in his *Gardeners' Dictionary* (1771) calls "the large-rooted Parsley, and which under cultivation develops both a parsnip-like, as well as a turnip-shaped form." Miller says, "This is now pretty commonly sold in the London markets, the roots being six times as large as the common Parsley. This sort was many years cultivated in Holland before the English gardeners could be prevailed upon to sow it. I brought the seeds of it from thence in 1727; but they refused to accept it, so that I cultivated it several years before it was known in the markets." At the present day the "long white" and the "round sugar" forms are sold by seed-growers and are in esteem for flavouring soups, stews, etc., the long variety being also cooked and eaten like parsnips, in taste resembling celeriac or turnip-rooted celery.

Neapolitan, or celery-leaved Parsley is grown for the use

of its leaf-stalks, which are blanched and eaten like those of celery.

The plain-leaved Parsley was the first known in this country, but it is not now much cultivated, the leaves being less attractive than those of the curled, of a less brilliant green and coarser in flavour. It also has too close a resemblance to Fool's Parsley, *Aethusa Cynapium,* a noxious weed of a poisonous nature, infesting gardens and fields. The leaves of the latter, though similar, and by the unobservant to be mistaken for the true Parsley, with unpleasant results, are, however, of a rather darker green and when bruised, emit an unpleasant odour, very different from that of Parsley. They are, also, more finely divided. When the two plants are in flower they are easily distinguished, *Aethusa* having three tiny, narrow, sharp-pointed leaflets hanging down under each little umbellule of the white umbel of flowers, whereas in the Garden Parsley, there is usually only one leaflet under the main umbel, the leaflets or bracts at the base of the small umbellules only being short and as fine as hairs. *Aethusa* leaves, also, are glossy beneath. Gerarde called *Aethusa* "Dog's Parsley," and says "the whole plant is of a naughty smell."

Like most biennials, Parsley develops only a rosette of leaves during the first year. During the second season, the erect, branched, grooved flower-stems are thrown up, a foot or more in height, bearing umbels of small greenish flowers. The fruits are light brown or grey, convex on one side and flat on the other, the convex side marked with fine ribs.

CULTIVATION. Parsley requires an ordinary, good, well-worked soil, but a moist one and a partially-shaded position is best. A little soot may be added to the soil.

The seed may be sown in drills, or broadcast, or, if only

to be used for culinary purposes, as edging, or between dwarf or short-lived crops.

For a continuous supply three sowings should be made: as early in February as the weather permits, in April or early in May, and in July and early August—the last being for the winter supply, in a sheltered position, with a southern exposure. Sow in February for the summer crop and for drying purposes. Seed sown then, however, takes several weeks to germinate, often as much as a full month, though germination may be hastened by a few days' soaking in tepid water.

The principal sowing is generally done in April: it then germinates more quickly and provides useful material for cutting throughout the summer. A mid-August sowing will furnish good plants for placing in cold frames for winter use.

An even broadcast sowing is preferable if the ground is in the condition to be trodden, which appears to fix the seed in its place, and after raking leaves a firm even surface.

The seed should be but slightly covered, not more than ½in. deep and thinly distributed; if in drills, these should be 1ft. apart.

It is not necessary, however (though usual), to sow the seed where the plants are to be grown, as when large enough, the seedlings can be pricked out into rows.

When the seedlings are well out of the ground—about an inch high—adequate thinning is imperative, as the plants dislike being cramped, and about 8ins. from plant to plant must be allowed; a well-grown plant will cover nearly a square foot of ground.

The rows should be liberally watered in dry weather; a sheltered position is preferred to a very exposed or open one, as the plants are liable to become burnt up in very hot and dry summers. The rows should be kept clean of weeds by hoeing, and frequent dressings of soot may be applied with advantage.

If the growth becomes coarse in the summer, cut off all the outer leaves and water well. This will induce a new growth of fine leaves again, and may always be done when the plants have grown to a good size, as it encourages a stocky growth.

When thus cut at the end of the summer, the plants will keep growing slowly, and the leaves made at this season will last all the winter in districts that are in any way favourable.

Soon after the old or last year's plants begin to grow again in the spring, they run away to flower, but if the flower stems are promptly removed, and the plants top-dressed and watered, they will remain productive for some time longer. Renew the beds every two years, as the plant dies down at the end of the second season.

When sowing Parsley to stand the winter, a plain-leaved variety will often be found superior to the curled or mossy sorts, which are, perhaps, handsomer, but the leaves retain both snow and rain, and when frost follows, the plants soon succumb. A plain-leaved Parsley is far hardier, and will survive even a severe winter and is equally good for cooking, though not so attractive for garnishing. Double the trouble is experienced in obtaining a supply of Parsley during the winter, when only the curled-leaved varieties are grown.

When curled Parsley is desired and is difficult to obtain, by there being no sufficiently sheltered spot in the garden for it, it may often be saved by placing a frame-light over the bed during severe weather to protect the plants, or they may be placed altogether in cold frames. Care must be taken with all parsley plants grown thus in frames, to pick off all decaying leaves directly noticed, and the soil should be stirred occasionally with a pointed stick between the plants, to prevent it becoming sour. Abundance of air should be given on all favourable occasions, removing the light altogether on fine days.

In field culture, if sown in drills 12-15ins. apart, 6 or 7lbs. of seed will be needed for the acre. For cultivation on a smaller scale, an ounce may be found sufficient for 50 to 100ft. of drill, which quantity should be enough for an ordinary family.

The first cutting of leaves from field-sown seed should be ready by mid-summer. A succession of cuttings can be obtained. About three weeks are required for a new crop of leaves to grow and mature after the plants have been cut. Larger yields can be secured by cutting only the fully-matured leaves, allowing the others to remain and develop for later cuttings, it being possible to gather three or four times as much from a given area in this way.

As Parsley is grown for its leaves, it can scarcely be over-fertilised, and to obtain the best results plenty of nitrogenous food must be in the soil, which should be well supplied with humus, preferably that derived from decaying leguminous crops, or from stable manure: a good compound manure may also be applied.

If it is desired to save the seed, the heads are cut when the bulk of the seed is brown, or at least dark coloured. The stalks must be cut carefully to avoid shaking the seed off. They are laid upon sheets of canvas and threshed very lightly, at once, to remove only the ripest seed. Then the stalks are spread thinly upon sheets in the sun for a couple of days, when they are threshed again, by which time, all the seed ripe enough to germinate will fall off. Spread both sets of seed thinly on sheets in an airy shed or loft, turning daily for 10 days or a fortnight, to make sure that they become perfectly dry, before storing in air-tight receptacles.

The uses of Parsley are many and by no means restricted to the culinary sphere. The most familiar employment of the leaves in their fresh state is, of course, finely-chopped, as a flavouring to sauces, soups, stuffings, rissoles, minces, etc., and also sprinkled over potatoes, whether mashed or whole, over vegetable marrow, or over salads, either potato salad or tomato salad. Sprigs of fresh Parsley form the most favourite garnish to cold dishes, and it is also often fried whole as a garnish. The leaves are extensively cultivated, not only for sending to market fresh, but also for the purpose of being dried and powdered as a culinary flavouring in winter, when only a limited supply of the fresh Parsley is obtainable. There is always a market for dried Parsley—as much as 2/- per lb. being given by wholesale buyers for first-class dried Parsley when demand is keen, though the usual price is 10d. to 1/- per lb.

In addition to the leaves, the STEMS are also dried and powdered, both as a culinary colouring and for dyeing purposes. There is a market for the seeds to supply nurserymen, etc., and the roots of the turnip-rooted variety, as above mentioned, are used as a vegetable and flavouring. Its imagined quality of destroying poison, to which Gerarde refers, was probably attributed to the plant from its remarkable power of overcoming strong scents, even the odour of garlic being rendered almost imperceptible when mingled with that of Parsley.

The plant is said to be fatal to small birds and a deadly poison to parrots, and also very injurious to fowls, but hares and rabbits will come from a great distance to indulge their taste for Parsley, so that it is scarcely possible to preserve it in gardens to which they have access. Sheep are also fond of it, and it has been said to be a sovereign remedy to preserve them from footrot, provided it be given them in sufficient quantities, about twice a week, for two or three hours each time, being recommended, but its beneficial action on this disease is nowadays not universally accepted.

To dry Parsley towards the close of the summer for culinary use, it may be put into the oven on muslin trays, when cooking is finished, this being repeated several times till thoroughly dry and crisp, when the leaves should be rubbed in the hands or through a coarse wire sieve and the powder then stored in tins, so that neither air nor light can reach it, or the good colour will not be preserved. In the trade there is a special method of drying which preserves the colour. Further particulars on the process of colour preservation can be obtained on application from the Author.

The oil is extracted from the "seeds," or rather fruits, when FRESH, in which condition, not dried, they are supplied to the manufacturing druggists.

Distillers have discovered a way of making imitation Absinthe from Parsley, and at one time in Paris bought up the whole available supply at prices often reaching as much as 16/- per lb.

PARSLEY SAUCE

Parsley for use in Parsley Sauce should never be chopped. Pick it from the stalks and place in a cup of boiling water, to which a pinch of soda and salt have been added. After leaving a moment or so, remove the Parsley and drop it into the melted butter you would use for the sauce. It will break into tiny shreds, and both odour and flavour are better than if chopped in the usual way.

PARSLEY PUREE

Take a handful of Parsley, put it in cold water with a little salt and a very small piece of soda, bring to the boil, then strain and mix with it ½oz. of butter, pound and add a few drops of Marshall's Sap Green, rub through the tammy and use.

A RECIPE FOR "PARSLEY PIE"
(From an old Cookery Book, 1863)

"Lay a fowl or a few bones of the scrag of veal seasoned, into a dish: scald a colander-full of picked parsley in milk; season, and add it to the fowl or meat, with a teacupful of any sort of good broth, or weak gravy. When it is baked, pour it into a quarter of a pint of cream, scalded, with the size of a walnut of butter, and a little flour. Shake it round to mix with the gravy already in.

"Lettuces, white mustard leaves, or spinach, may be added to the Parsley, and scalded before being put in."

ANOTHER RECIPE FOR PARSLEY SAUCE

Melt two ounces of butter in a clean pan, then sprinkle in from one to two ounces of flour, according to the richness desired, and stir this over the fire till the butter is quite melted and the flour has been absorbed, so that a smooth paste is formed which can be lifted clean from the pan, then add gradually half a pint of water, stirring this steadily the whole time; when the water is all added, put in a sufficient quantity of well-chopped Parsley and let it boil from ten to twelve minutes, stirring to ensure the flour being well cooked, and use.

ROSEMARY

(N.O. LABIATÆ)

ROSMARINUS OFFICINALIS Linn.
Local Name: Rosemary.

USES

LEAVES, STEMS, and FLOWERS used for flavouring; also in Claret cup, etc.
OIL distilled from plant.

Rosemary, the well-known evergreen shrub, grown in small quantities in almost every garden, was introduced into England before the Norman Conquest. It came originally from the south of Europe, where it grows abundantly on the dry, rocky hills of the Mediterranean region.

The shrub takes its name from *ros,* dew, and *marinus,* belonging to the sea, in allusion to the grey, glistening appearance of the plant and its natural locality near the sea, with somewhat of its odour.

The ancients are well acquainted with this shrub, which has always been supposed to strengthen the memory. On this account it became the emblem of fidelity in lovers. It holds quite a special position among the herbs from the symbolism attached to it, apart from any of its household or medicinal uses. Not only was it in olden days employed at weddings, but also at funerals, for decking churches and banqueting halls at festivals, as incense in religious ceremonies, and in spells against magic—in fact, it was always regarded with a species of affection perhaps given to no other plant.

"There's Rosemary for you, that's for remembrance! Pray

you, love, remember," says Ophelia in *Hamlet*.

At weddings, it was entwined in the wreath worn by the bride, being first dipped into scented water. Anne of Cleves, we are told, wore such a wreath at her wedding. A Rosemary branch, richly gilded and tied with silken ribands of all colours, was also presented to the wedding guests, as a symbol of love and loyalty. Together with an orange stuck with cloves it often served as a little New Year's gift—allusions to this custom are to be found in Ben Jonson's plays.

Sir Thomas More writes: "As for Rosmarine, I lett it runne all over my garden walls, not onlie because my bees love it, but because it is the herb sacred to remembrance, and, therefore, to friendship; whence a sprig of it hath a dumb language that maketh it the chosen emblem of our funeral wakes and in our buriall grounds."

In place of more costly incense, the ancients often employed Rosemary in their religious ceremonies. An old French name for it was *Incensier*.

Rosemary was called *Libanotis coronaria,* and this the Arabs translated into *akleel-al-jibbul,* or "Mountain Crown."

The flavour of Narbonne Honey is supposed to be due to the bees feeding on the flowers of Rosemary.

It was an old custom to burn Rosemary in sick chambers, because of its supposed preservative powers against pestilential disorders. In the French hospitals it is customary to burn Rosemary, together with Juniper berries, for purifying the air and preventing infection. Like Rue, it was placed in the dock of courts of justice, to guard those present from the contagion of gaol-fever that might have been brought in by the prisoner.

In early times, Rosemary was freely cultivated in kitchen-gardens and came to represent the dominant influence of the house mistress. "Where Rosemary flourished, the woman ruled." Sprigs of the shrub were formerly stuck into beef, whilst being roasted, as a relish and used as a seasoning for poultry.

It was cultivated by the Spaniards in the thirteenth century, and from the fifteenth to the eighteenth century was popular as a condiment with salt meats, but has since declined in popularity, until now it is used for seasoning almost exclusively in Italian, French, Spanish and German cookery.

DESCRIPTION. The plant is a half-hardy evergreen growing 2ft. or more high, the erect, branching, woody stems bearing a profusion of little, narrow, blunt leaves, less than an inch long, with their margins turned back, their surfaces dark green above and hoary white beneath. The leaves have a pungently aromatic and somewhat camphoraceous odour. The flowers are arranged in leafy clusters in the upper parts of the stem, and are small and pale blue; much of the active volatile principle resides in their calyces, though all parts of the plant are fragrant.

There are varieties with silver- and gold-striped leaves, but the green-leaved variety is the kind used medicinally and for the extraction of the oil, obtained by distillation from its flowering tops. The blossoms contain much nectar, and the famous Narbonne Honey is said to derive its flavour from Rosemary, which grows there in great profusion.

CULTIVATION. Rosemary is propagated by seeds, cuttings and layers, and also by division of roots. Seeds may be sown upon a warm, sunny border in February or March.

Cuttings, taken in August, 6ins. long, and dibbled into a shady border, two-thirds of their length in the ground, under a hand glass, will root and be ready for transplanting into permanent quarters the following autumn. Layering may be readily accomplished in summer by bringing some of the lower branches down and pegging them beneath a little sandy soil.

Rosemary succeeds best in a light, rather dry soil, and in a sheltered situation, such as the base of a low wall with a south aspect. On a chalk soil it grows smaller, but is more fragrant. The silver- and gold-striped kinds are not quite so hardy.

The finest plants are said to be raised from seed.

The tender fresh leaves and stems and the flowers have been used for flavouring stews, fish and meat sauces. They may also be used in small quantities for summer cups, such as cider cup and claret cup, and a small pinch is also agreeable in salads.

Rosemary Wine was of old always kept in the still-room, as it was considered, when taken in small quantities, to act as a quieting cordial to a weak heart subject to palpitation. It is made by chopping up sprigs of green Rosemary, pouring on them white wine, which is strained off after a few days and is then ready for use. By stimulating the brain and nervous system, it is a good remedy for headaches caused by a feeble circulation.

MOTH DESTROYER

½lb. dried Rosemary
½lb.   „   Mint
¼lb.   „   Tansy
¼lb.   „   Thyme
2 tablespoonfuls fresh ground cloves.

Mix well together and store in well-closed box. Scatter lavishly among fur, blankets, and clothing as they are stored and no moth will go near them.

(From *Garden of Ignorance, by* Marian Cran.)

"A handful of sliced Horseradish root, with a handsome little faggot of Rosemary, Thyme, and Winter Savoury" is recommended in the directions for dressing a trout, in Cotton's sequel to Izaak Walton's *Compleat Angler* (1676).

RUE

(N.O. RUTACEÆ)

RUTA GRAVEOLENS Linn.
   Local Name: Rue.

USES

YOUNG LEAVES sometimes used in Claret Cup.

Rue, a hardy evergreen, somewhat shrubby plant, is a native of Southern Europe. It is a member of the same botanical family as the orange, and unrelated to most of the other herbs with which we are dealing.

It had a high reputation for seasoning and as a medicine in the times of the Greeks and Romans—in Pliny's time it was considered to be curative in no less than 84 maladies.

The name *Ruta* is from the Greek *reuo,* to set free, because this herb is so efficacious in various diseases. It was much used by the ancients; Hippocrates specially commended it, and it constituted a chief ingredient of the famous antidote to poison used by Mithridates. In this country Rue is one of our oldest garden plants, cultivated for its use medicinally, having, together with other herbs, been introduced by the Romans, but it is not found in a wild state.

At one time the holy water was sprinkled from brushes made of Rue at the ceremony usually preceding the Sunday celebration of High Mass, for which reason it is supposed it was named the Herb of Repentance and the Herb of Grace. "There's Rue for you and here's some for me; we may call it herb of grace o' Sundays," says Ophelia in *Hamlet*.

Rue has been regarded from the earliest times as most successful in warding off contagion and preventing the attacks of fleas and other noxious insects. It was the custom —lasting into the early part of last century—for Judges, sitting at Assizes, to have sprigs of Rue placed on the bench of the dock, as defensive against the pestilential infection brought into court from gaol by the prisoner. The bouquet still presented in some districts to Judges at the Assizes was originally a bunch of aromatic herbs, given to him for the like purpose of warding off the gaol-fever, and Rue formed a portion of it.

Recent research has shown that the essential oil contained in Rue, as in other aromatic herbs like Elecampane, Rosemary and Cinnamon, serves by its germicidal principles to extinguish bacterial life.

DESCRIPTION. The stem is woody at the lower part and much branched, 18ins. to 2ft. high, bearing small, oblong, stalked leaves, bluish-green and shining, two or three times divided, the terminal leaflet broader and notched at the end. The rather large greenish-yellow flowers are in terminal panicles, and are in bloom from June to September. The whole plant has a very powerful, disagreeable odour, and an exceedingly bitter, acid and nauseous taste.

CULTIVATION. The plant grows almost anywhere, but thrives best in a partially sheltered and dry situation. Propagation may be effected: (1) by seeds, sown outside, broadcast, in spring, raked in and the beds kept free from weeds, the seedlings, when about 2ins. high, being transplanted into fresh beds, allowing about 18ins. each way, as the plants become bushy; (2) by cuttings, taken in spring and inserted for a time, until well rooted, in a shady border; (3) by rooted slips, also taken in spring. Every slip or cutting of the young wood will readily grow, and this is the most expeditious way of raising a stock.

Rue will live much longer and is less liable to be injured by frost in winter when grown in a poor, dry, rubbishy soil than in good ground.

As the flowers are attractive, Rue is often planted in shrubberies for ornamental purposes. When so grown it is well to cut the stems close to the ground every two or three years.

Rue is no longer used as a seasoning, but it is still used to a limited extent by some who like bitter flavours, not only in culinary preparations, but in beverages, its young leaves being occasionally put into claret cup. Italians use the leaves as a salad.

Country people use Rue leaves as a cure for croup in poultry, either boiling them in treacle, thus making a conserve of them, or chopping them fine, mixing them with butter, and administering them in the form of little pills. Rue has also been employed in the diseases of cattle.

A few sprigs of Rue hung in a room will keep flies from the apartment.

SAGE

(N.O. LABIATÆ)

SALVIA OFFICINALIS Linn.
Local Name: Garden Sage.

USES

LEAVES as flavouring, seasoning, and as substitute for tea. As a country wine; for perfumery—scenting soaps and sachets. As an ingredient in Herb Beer. In cheesemaking.

The Common Sage, belonging to the order *Labiatæ,* the familiar plant of the kitchen-garden, an evergreen under-shrub, though not a native of these islands, its natural habitat being the northern shores of the Mediterranean, has been cultivated for culinary and medicinal purposes for many centuries in England, France and Germany, being sufficiently hard to stand any ordinary winter outside. Gerarde mentions it as being in 1597 a well-known herb in English gardens and represented in his own garden in Holborn by several varieties.

Sage is found in its natural wild condition from Spain along the Mediterranean coast up to and including the east side of the Adriatic; it grows in profusion on the mountains and hills in Croatia and Dalmatia, being found mostly where there is a limestone formation with very little soil, but it seems to grow in all kinds of places, some of the barren hills in the region of Fiume having very little vegetation other than this wild Sage. When wild it is much like the common garden Sage, though more shrubby in appearance and has a more penetrating odour, being more bitterly spicy and astringent than the cultivated plant. The best kind, it is stated, grows on the islands of Veglia and Cherso, near Fiume, where the surrounding district is known as the Sage region. The collection of Sage forms an important cottage industry in Dalmatia. During its blooming season, moreover, the bees gather the nectar and genuine Sage honey commands there the highest price, owing to its flavour.

The name of the genus, *Salvia,* is derived from the Latin, *Salvere,* to be saved, in reference to the curative properties of the plant, which was in olden times celebrated as a medicinal herb of great value. This name was corrupted popularly to *Sauja* and *Sauge* (the French form), in old English, "Sawge," which has become our present-day name of Sage.

Sage is now neglected by the regular medical practitioner, though still used in domestic medicine, as a homely remedy. It was otherwise among the ancients, among whom and throughout the Middle Ages, it was in high repute. A well-known monkish line about it runs: *Cur moriatur homo cui Salvia crescit in horto?* ("Why should a man die whilst sage grows in his garden?") corresponding to an old English saying:

> "He that would live for aye
> Must eat Sage in May."

A translation of an old French saying runs:—

> "Sage helps the nerves and by its powerful might
> Palsy is cured and fever put to flight,"

and Gerarde, clearly believing this, says: "Sage is singularly good for the head and brain, it quickeneth the senses and memory, strengtheneth the sinews, restoreth health to those that have the palsy, and taketh away shakey trembling of the members." He says further: "No man need to doubt of the wholesomeness of *Sage Ale,* being brewed as it should be with Sage, Betony, Scabious, Spikenard, Squinnette and Fennell Seed."

Sage generally grows about a foot or more high, with wiry stems. The leaves are set in pairs on the stem and are 1½–2ins. long, stalked, oblong, rounded at the ends, finely wrinkled by a strongly-marked network of veins on both sides, greyish-green in colour, softly hairy and beneath glandular. The flowers are in whorls, purplish and the corollas lipped. They blossom in August. All parts of the plant have a strong, scented odour and a warm, bitter, somewhat astringent taste, due to the volatile oil contained in the tissues.

In cultivation, Sage is a very variable species, and in gardens may be found varieties with narrower leaves, crisped, red, or variegated leaves and smaller or white flowers. The form of the calyx teeth also varies and the tube of the corolla is sometimes much longer. The two usually absent upper stamens are sometimes present in very small sterile hooks. The Red Sage and the Broad-leaved variety of the White (or Green) Sage—both of which are used and have been proved to be the best for medicinal purposes—and the narrow-leaved White Sage, which is best for *culinary* purposes as a seasoning, are classed merely as varieties of *Salvia officinalis,* not as separate species. There is a variety called the Spanish, or Lavender-leaved Sage, and another called the Wormwood Sage, which is very frequent.

CULTIVATION. The Garden Sage succeeds best in a warm and rather dry border, but will grow well almost anywhere in ordinary garden soil; it thrives in a situation somewhat shaded from sunshine, but not strictly under trees.

It is a hardy plant, but though a perennial, does not last above three or four years without degenerating, so that the plantation should be renewed at least every four years. It is propagated occasionally by seed, but more frequently by cuttings. New plantations are readily made by pulling off the young shoots from three-year-old plants in spring, generally in the latter end of April, as soon as ever they attain a sufficiency of hardness to enable them to maintain themselves on the moisture of the ground and atmosphere while the lower extremities are preparing roots. If advantage be taken of any showery weather that may occur, there is little touble in obtaining any required number of plants, which may either be struck in the bed where they are to grow, inserting a foot apart each way, or in some other shady spot whence they may be removed to permanent quarters when rooted. The latter plan is the best when the weather is too bright and sunny to expect Sage to strike well in its ordinary quarters. See the young plants do not suffer from want of water during their first summer and hoe the rows regularly to induce a bushy growth, nipping off the growing tips if shooting up too tall. Treat the ground with soot and mulch in winter with old manure. Cuttings may also be taken in the autumn, as soon as the plants have ceased flowering.

Sage is also very often propagated by layers, in the spring and autumn, the branches of old plants being pegged down on the ground and covered with half an inch of earth. The plant being like other of the woody-stemmed garden herbs, a "stem rooter," each of the stems thus covered will produce quantities of rootlets from just lying in contact with the ground and can after a time be cut away from the old plant and transplanted to other quarters as a separate plant. Young plants or young rooted growths are found at the base of old, apparently dead shoots of Sage: these growths can be severed from the parent and a new plantation formed.

Red Sage is always propagated by layering or by cuttings, as the seed does not produce a red-leaved plant, but reverts back to the original green-leaved type, though efforts are being made to insure the production of a Red Sage that shall set seed that shall remain true and develop into the red-leaved plant. When grown on a commercial scale, and sown in drills at the rate of two seeds to the inch, and in rows 15ins. apart, about 8lbs. of seed will be needed to the acre.

At the present day by far the largest demand for Sage is for culinary use, and it should pay to grow it in quantity for this purpose as it is little trouble. For this, the White Variety, with somewhat pale green leaves should be taken.

The strength and fineness of the flavour depend mostly upon the harvesting and drying. For drying, the leaves are cut when the flowers appear. Sage is dried in bunches like the other woody-stemmed sweet herbs, care being taken to pick only on a dry day, and to strip off all stained and insect-eaten leaves.

When properly dried the properties of the plant are in a great measure retained, but Sage should not be kept long in a dried state, not longer than one year, as it rapidly deteriorates.

It is estimated that 9lbs. of fresh leaves produce 2lbs. of the dried herb.

Sage has been medicinally employed in many ways, even though in this country it has fallen into disuse in regular official practice.

The infusion when made for *internal* use is termed Sage Tea, and can be made simply by pouring 1 pint of boiling water on to 1oz. of the dried herb, the dose being from a wineglassful to half a tea-cupful, as often as required, but the old-fashioned way of making it is more elaborate, and the result is quite a pleasant drink, very cooling in fevers, and also a cleanser and purifier of the blood. Half an ounce of fresh Sage leaves, 1oz. of sugar, the juice of one lemon, or ¼oz. of grated rind, and infused in a quart of boiling water and strained off after half an hour. (In Jamaica, the negroes use as a cooling drink in fevers Sage Tea made from the leaves of this Sage, sweetened, and flavoured with Lime juice, instead of lemon.)

Sage Tea or infusion of Sage is a valuable agent in the delirium of fevers and in the nervous excitement frequently accompanying brain and nervous diseases.

The fresh leaves, rubbed on the teeth, will cleanse them and strengthen the gums.

Sage and Onion stuffing for ducks and geese and for pork is well known, being eaten with them as the bitter and condimentary pungency of the herb enables the stomach better to digest the rich, luscious, oily meat. A few less familiar recipes may, however, be of interest, taken mostly from cookery books of a former generation.

Here is an old recipe in Warner's *Ancient Cookery*, 1791, for "Sawgeat," Sawge, as stated above, being an old form of the name Sage.

SAWGEAT. Take Pork and seeth (boil) it wel and grinde it smale and medle (mingle) it with ayren (eggs) and ygrated (grated) brede (bread). Do thereto salt sprinkled and saffron. Take a close litull ball of it in foiles (leaves) of Sawge. Wet it with a bator (batter) of ayren, fry and serve forth.

In *The Cook's Oracle*, 1821, there is a good recipe for: SAGE AND ONION SAUCE. Chop very fine an ounce of onion and half an ounce of green Sage leaves, put them in a stamper with four spoonsful of water, simmer gently for 10 minutes, then put in a teaspoonful of pepper and salt and one ounce of fine bread-crumbs. Mix well together, then pour to it ¼ pint of Broth, Gravy or Melted Butter, stir well together and simmer a few minutes longer. This is a relishing sauce for Roast Pork, Geese or Duck, or with Green Peas on Maigre Days.

The same book gives: A RELISH FOR ROAST PORK OR GOOSE. 2ozs. of leaves of Green Sage, an oz. of fresh lemon peel, pared thin, same of salt, minched shallot and half a drachm of Cayenne pepper, ditto of Citric acid, steeped for a fortnight in a pint of Claret. Shake it well every day; let it stand a day to settle and decant the clear liquid. Bottle it and cork it close. Use a tablespoonful or more in a quarter of a pint of gravy or melted butter.

Another modern Sage sauce, excellent with roast pork: SAGINA SAUCE. Take 6 large Sage leaves, 2 onions, 1 teaspoonful of flour, 1 teaspoonful of vinegar, butter the size of a walnut, salt, pepper, and ½ pint of good brown gravy. Scald the Sage leaves and chop them with the onions to a mince-meat. Put them in a stew-pan with the butter, sprinkle in the flour, cover close and steam 10 minutes. Then add the vinegar, gravy and seasoning, and simmer half an hour.

In Walsh's *Manual of Domestic Economy,* 1857, is the following recipe for: SAGE CHEESE. Bruise the tops of young red Sage in a mortar with some leaves of spinach and squeeze the juice; mix it with the rennet in the milk, more or less, according to the preferred colour and taste. When the curd is come, break it gently and put it in with the skimmer till it is pressed 2ins above the vat. Press it 8 or 10 hours. Salt it and turn every day.

Many kinds of Sage have been used as substitutes for tea, the Chinese having been said to prefer Sage Tea to their own native product, and at one time bartering for it with the Dutch, giving thrice the quantity of their choicest tea in exchange. It is recorded that George Whitfield, when at Oxford in 1733, lived wholesomely, if sparingly, on a diet of Sage Tea alone, sugar and coarse bread. Balsamic Sage, *Salvia grandiflora,* a broad-leaved Sage with many-flowered whorls of blossoms, used to be preferred to all others for making tea. An infusion of Speedwell (*Veronica officinalis*), Sage and Wood Betony together is said to make an excellent beverage for breakfast, as a substitute for tea, Speedwell having somewhat the flavour of Chinese green tea. In Holland, the leaves of *Salvia glutinosa,* the Yellow-flowered Hardy Sage, both flowers and foliage of which exhale a pleasant odour, are used to give flavour to country wines.

It was formerly thought that Sage used in the making of Cheese improved its flavour, and in a passage of a poem of Gay, "Marbled with Sage, the hardening cheese she pressed," we find a reference to this custom, which no doubt was a wholesome one, the volatile oil in the Sage leaves acting as a corrective to the richness of the cheese, in the same way that it is of use when Sage forms an ingredient of stuffings and sauces taken with rich meat.

Italian peasants eat Sage as a preservative of health and many of our own country people often eat the leaves with bread and butter, than which, it has been said, there is no better and more wholesome way of taking it.

A species of Sage, *Salvia pomifera,* the Apple-bearing Sage, of a very peculiar growth, is common on some of the Greek islands. It has a firm, fleshy protuberance of about ¾ in. thickness, swelling out from the branches of the plant and supposed to be produced in the same manner as oak-apples, by the puncture of an insect of the *Cynips* genus. These excrescences are semi-transparent like jelly. They are called Sage Apples, and under that name are to be met with in the markets as an article of ordinary sale. They are candied with sugar and made into a kind of sweetmeat and conserve which is regarded as a great delicacy by the Greeks, and is said to possess healing and salutary qualities. It has an agreeable and astringent flavour. This plant is considerably larger than the common Sage of our gardens, and its flavour and smell are much more powerful, being somewhat like a mixture of Lavender and Sage. It grows very abundantly in Candia, Syros and Crete, where it attains to the size of a small shrub. The leaves are collected annually, dried and used medicinally as an infusion.

Another South European species, an annual, *Salvia Horminum,* the Red-topped Sage, has its whorls of flowers terminated by clusters of small purple or red leaves, being for this peculiarity often grown in gardens as an ornamental plant. The leaves and seed of this species, put into the vat while fermenting, greatly increase the inebriating quality of the liquor. An infusion of the leaves has been considered a good gargle for sore gums, and a powder of them to make a good snuff.

Certain varieties of Sage seeds are mucilaginous and nutritive, and are used in Mexico by the Indians as a food, under the name of *Chia*.

Eaten to excess, Sage is poisonous.

STUFFING FOR POULTRY AND PORK

Peel and cut six onions into quarters, and boil until half cooked; then drain and chop finely, adding a piece of butter and an equal quantity of bread-crumbs, one good-sized teaspoonful of powdered Sage, a small quantity of chopped Parsley, add salt and pepper to taste, and a little sugar. Mix thoroughly.

SUMMER SAVORY

WINTER SAVORY

(N.O. Labiatæ)

Satureia hortensis Linn.
  Local Name: Summer Savory.
Satureia montana Linn.
  Local Name: Winter Savory.

USES

Leaves for many culinary purposes. Dried leaves to make syrups and conserves.

The genus Satureia (the old Latin name used by Pliny), of the order *Labiatæ,* comprises about 14 species of highly aromatic, hardy herbs or under-shrubs, all, except one species, being natives of the Mediterranean region.

Several species have been introduced into England, but only two, the annual Summer or Garden Savory and the perennial Winter Savory, are generally grown. The annual is more usually grown, but the leaves of both are employed in cookery, like other sweet herbs, the leaves and tender tops being used with Marjoram and Thyme to season dressings for turkey, veal or fish.

Both species were noticed by Virgil as being among the most fragrant of herbs, and on this account recommended to be grown near beehives. There is reason to suppose that they were cultivated in remote ages, before the East Indian spices were known and in common use. Vinegar, flavoured with Savory and other aromatic herbs, was used by the Romans in the same manner as Mint sauce is by us.

In Shakespeare's time, Savory was a familiar herb, for we find it mentioned, together with the Mints, Marjoram and Lavender, in *The Winter's Tale.*

Description. Summer Savory is a hardy, downy annual, with slender erect stems about a foot high. It flowers in July, having pale lilac labiate flowers, in small axillary clusters, on short stalks or pedicels, sometimes in groups of three. The leaves about ½in. long, are entire, oblong, linear, acute, narrowed at the base into a short leaf-stalk, often fassicled— *i.e.,* in little bunches or groups. The hairs on the stem are short and decurved. The whole plant is very fragrant.

Cultivation. Summer Savory is raised from seeds, sown early in April, in shallow drills, 9ins. or a foot apart. Select a sunny situation and thin out the seedlings, when large enough, to 6ins. apart in the rows. It likes a rich, light soil.

The seeds may also be sown broadcast, when they must be thinned out, the thinned out seedlings being planted in another bed at 6ins. distance from each other and well watered. The seeds are very slow in germinating.

The early spring seedlings may be first topped for fresh use in June. When the flower-buds appear, the stems may be cut off and hung up to dry for future use, in the usual way (see p. 18). The cut-down plants will continue to produce fresh shoots, and these may be gathered later on.

As a kitchen herb, Savory, which has a distinctive taste, though it somewhat recalls that of Marjoram, is not only added to stuffings, pork-pies and sausages, but also to stews and sauces used with such meats as veal, pork, duck and goose. Sprigs of it, fresh, may be boiled with broad beans and green peas, in the same manner as Mint is employed. It is also boiled with dried peas in making pea-soup. For garnishing it has been used as a substitute for Parsley and Chervil. Savory has aromatic and carminative properties, and though chiefly used as a culinary herb, it may be added to medicines for its aromatic and warming qualities. It was formerly deemed a sovereign remedy for the colic. Culpepper thought highly of them, and tells us: "Keep it dry by you all the year, if you love yourself and your ease, and it is a hundred pounds to a penny if you do not," and goes on to enumerate certain complaints for which it may be used as a remedy. He considered Summer Savory better than Winter Savory for drying to make conserves and syrups.

Winter Savory is a dwarf, hardy, perennial, glabrous or slightly pubescent under-shrub, also a native of Southern Europe. The stems are woody at the base, 12 to 18ins. high, much branched and spreading. The leaves are oblong, linear and acute, the lower ones often wedge-shaped and obtuse. The flowers in bloom in June are very pale purple or pinkish, and are arranged in spikes or racemes.

CULTIVATION. It is propagated either from seeds, sown at a similar period and in the same manner as Summer Savory, or from cuttings and divisions of root. It is woodier and more bushy than Summer Savory.

Cuttings formed of young side shoots, with a heel attached, may be taken in April or June, and will readily root under a hand-glass, or in a shady border outside.

Divisions of the roots should be made in March or April, and plants obtained in this way, or from cuttings, should be permanently inserted during a showery period in the latter part of summer, in rows, at the distance of 1ft. apart.

The plant grows better in a poor, stony soil than a rich one. In a rich soil, plants take in too much moisture to stand the severity of our winter. In the soil that suits it, Winter Savory makes a good-sized shrub. It will continue for several years, but when the plants are old the shoots are short and not so well furnished with leaves. It is, therefore, well to raise a supply of young plants every other year.

For drying, the first cutting may be secured during July, the second in late August or September.

USES. Parkinson tells us that Winter Savory used to be dried and powdered and mixed with grated bread-crumbs "to breade their meate, be it fish or flesh, to give it a quicker relish." It is recommended by older writers, together with other herbs, in the dressing of trout.

When dried, it is used as seasoning in the same manner as Summer Savory, but is considered inferior in flavour. It is not employed medicinally.

Both the old authorities and modern gardeners agree that a sprig of either of the Savories rubbed on wasp- and bee-stings gives instant relief.

SATUREIA THYMBRA, which is used in Spain as a spice and

is closely allied to the Savories grown in English kitchen-gardens, yields an oil containing about 12 per cent of Thymol. Other species of Satureia contain Carvacrol. The oil from Summer Savory contains 30 per cent of Carvacrol, and that from Winter Savory still more. (See special pamphlet on Thyme.)

A HERB MIXTURE

Take equal proportions of Knotted Marjoram and Winter Savory, with half the quantity of Basil, Thyme, and Tarragon, all rubbed to powder and keep in a closely corked bottle. This is to be recommended for use in forcemeat and for flavouring.

ANOTHER AROMATIC HERB SEASONING

This is useful as a flavouring in winter for purée of cabbage, preserved French beans, soups, and sauces:—

1oz. nutmegs
1oz. mace
2ozs. cloves
1oz. dried bay leaves
3ozs. dried basil
3ozs. dried marjoram
2ozs. dried winter savory
3ozs. dried thyme
¼oz. cayenne pepper
½oz. grated lemon-peel
2 cloves of garlic.

Mix, pulverize, sift, and store as in previous recipe.

SALAD VINEGAR

A very good Salad Vinegar can be made of 3ozs. each of Tarragon, Savory, Chives, Eschallots, a handful of the tops of Mint and Balm, all dried and pounded. Put into a wide-mouthed bottle or stone jar with a gallon of the best vinegar. Cork closely, set in the sun for a fortnight, strain, press all the juice and vinegar from the herbs. Let it stand a day to settle, then strain through a filtering-bag.

SOUP-HERB VINEGAR

This is made of ½oz. each of Lemon Thyme, Winter Savory, Sweet Marjoram, and Sweet Basil, 2 drachms of lemon-peel and eschallots, 1 drachm of celery seed, infused for 10 days in a pint of best vinegar.

SOUTHERNWOOD

(N.O. Compositæ)

Artemisia Abrotanum Linn.
Local Names: Southernwood, Old Man, Lad's Love.

USES

Leaves said to keep moths from attacking clothes.

Southernwood is a woody-stemmed perennial, belonging to the order *Compositæ* a native of the South of Europe, indigenous in Spain and Italy.

It is a familiar and favourite plant in our gardens, growing about a couple of feet high, though it rarely flowers in our gardens, and the peculiar affection with which this little shrub—with its finely-divided, greyish-green leaves—is regarded is somewhat difficult to explain. It was introduced into this country in 1548, and there are few gardens in which a root or two of "Old Man" or "Lad's Love" (to quote two of its popular names) may not be found.

The leaves have a fragrant, highly aromatic odour, that is somewhat lemon-like. This odour is dependent on the volatile oil contained in the plant. The scent is said to be disagreeable to bees, and also to other insects, for which reason the French call the plant GARDEROBE, as moths will not attack clothes among which it is laid.

In Italy, Southernwood is employed as a culinary herb, the young shoots being used for flavouring cakes and other culinary preparations.

TANSY

(N.O. Compositæ)

TANACETUM VULGARE Linn.
     Local Name: Tansy.

USES

LEAVES, shredded, as a culinary flavouring.

Tansy, a composite plant very familiar in our hedgerows and waste places, is a hardy perennial, widely spread over Europe.

The stem is erect and leafy, about 2–3ft. high, grooved and

angular. The leaves are alternate, much cut into, 2–6ins. long and about 4ins. wide. The plant is conspicuous in August and September by its heads of round, flat, dull yellow flowers, growing in clusters, which earn it the name of "Buttons." It has a very curious, and not altogether disagreeable odour, somewhat like camphor.

It is often naturalised in our gardens for ornamental cultivation. The feathery leaves of the Wild Tansy are beautiful, especially when growing in abundance on marshy ground, and it has a more refreshing scent than the Garden Tansy.

The name Tansy is probably derived from the Greek *Athanasia,* which signifies immortality, either, says Dodoens, because it lasts so long in flower, or as Ambrosius thought, because it is so capital for preserving dead bodies from corruption. It was said to have been given to Ganymede to make him immortal.

CULTIVATION. Tansy will thrive in almost any soil and may be increased, either in spring or autumn, by slips or by dividing the creeping roots, which, if permitted to remain undisturbed, will, in a short time, overspread the ground. When transplanting the slips or portions of root, place therefore at least a foot apart.

Although the leaves have an acrid, bitter taste, they have been used, shredded, for flavouring puddings, cakes, omelettes, salads, stews and other culinary dishes. "This balsamic plant," said Boerhaave, the great Danish physician of the eighteenth century, "will supply the place of nutmeg and cinnamon." Gerarde tells us that Tansy Teas were highly esteemed in Lent, as well as Tansy puddings.

Tansy is connected with some interesting old customs observed at Easter time, when, says the old Chronicler, the clergy of some churches, even the Archbishops and Bishops, were wont to play at handball with men of their congregation, and a Tansy cake was the reward of the victors. These Tansy cakes were made from the young leaves of the plant, mixed with eggs, and were thought to purify the humours of the body after the limited fare of Lent. In time, this custom obtained a kind of symbolism, and Tansies, as these cakes were called, came to be eaten on Easter Day as a remembrance of the bitter herbs eaten by the Jews at the Passover. Coles (1656) says the origin of eating it in the spring is because Tansy is very wholesome after the salt fish consumed during Lent, and counteracts the ill-effects which the "moist and cold constitution of winter has made on people."

Tansy has of old sometimes been added to a salad, but its flavour is too overpowering to allow of any but a very sparing use.

J. T. Burgess, in *English Wild Flowers,* says:—

"In Ireland the flavour of the tansy is much liked, and is used specially in the flavouring of the Cork luxury, *drisheens,* immortalized by Lady Morgan."

TARRAGON

(N.O. Compositæ)

Artemisia Dracunculus Linn.
  Local Name: Tarragon.

USES

Leaves used to temper the coolness of other herbs in salads; and to flavour fish sauces. Used also to make tarragon vinegar.

Tarragon, a member of the composite tribe, closely allied to Wormwood, as a fairly hardy, herbaceous, rather shrubby perennial—a native of southern Russia, Siberia and Tartary, and cultivated for the last 500 years in Europe for the use of its aromatic leaves and tender shoots. Tarragon is more common in Continental than in English cookery, and has long been cultivated in France for culinary purposes.

The name Tarragon is a corruption of the French *Esdragon,* derived from the Latin *Dracunculus,* a little dragon, which also serves as its specific name. It was of old sometimes called little Dragon Mugwort, and in French has also the name *Herbe au Dragon.* To this, as to other Dragon herbs was ascribed the faculty of curing the bites and stings of venomous beasts and of mad dogs. The name is practically the same in most countries, though no real reason for the title is known.

DESCRIPTION. The plant has numerous branching stems, which grow to a height of about 2ft. and bear long, narrow leaves, which unlike other members of its genus, are undivided. It blossoms in August, the small flowers, in round heads, being yellow mingled with black, and rarely fully open. The roots are long and fibrous, spreading by runners.

CULTIVATION. Two kinds of Tarragon are cultivated in kitchen gardens: the French Tarragon with very smooth, dark green leaves and the true Tarragon flavour, which is a native of the South of Europe, and Russian Tarragon, a native of Siberia, with less smooth leaves of a fresher green shade and somewhat lacking in the peculiar tartness of the French variety.

As Tarragon rarely produces fertile flowers, either in England or France, it is not often raised by seed, but it may be readily propagated by division of roots in March or April, or by cuttings struck in a little warmth when growth is commencing in spring or later in the summer, under a hand-glass, placed outside. A few young plants should be raised annually to keep up a supply.

When transplanting, divide clumps into small portions and pull to pieces with the hand, but do not chip them into sections with the spade, or you will damage the roots. Plant the pieces a foot apart each way, and leave them undisturbed for four years. As they spread a good deal, they will soon cover the ground freely.

Tarragon loves warmth and sunshine, and succeeds best in warm, rather dry situations, and a little protection should also be afforded the roots through the winter, as during severe frost they are liable to be injured. Both varieties need a dry, rather poor soil, for if set in a moist soil, they are likely to be killed by our winter.

The green leaves should be picked between Midsummer and Michaelmas. The foliage may also be cut and dried in early autumn for use in a dry state afterwards. The beds should then be entirely cut down and top-dressed to protect from frost.

Sometimes strong young plants planted in a sheltered border from October to December, will produce green shoots all through the winter if the frost be not too severe, but as a rule, if green leaves are required during winter, a few roots should be lifted in the autumn and placed in heat: it will require but a small quantity to maintain a succession.

The leaves are generally used in the fresh condition, but may be dried in the usual way in bunches, if desired. For this purpose they are gathered in midsummer. A second cutting made be made in late September or early October.

John Evelyn, in his treatise on salads, says of Tarragon: " 'Tis highly cordial and friends to the head, heart and liver."

In Continental cookery its use is advised to temper the

coolness of other herbs in salads. The leaves, which have a fragrant smell in addition to their aromatic taste, are also used, especially by the French, with stews, steaks and other meat preparations. They are often employed as an ingredient in pickles. Tarragon forms also an excellent flavouring for fish sauces. Perhaps the most popular way it is employed is as a decoction in vinegar. Vinegars used in former times frequently to be aromatised by steeping in them Rosemary, Gilliflowers and Barberries, but Tarragon is the only herb now used in this manner.

To make Tarragon vinegar, fill a wide-mouthed bottle with the freshly-gathered leaves, picked just before the herb flowers, on a dry day. Pick the leaves off the stalks and dry a little before the fire. Then place in a jar, cover with the best vinegar, allow to stand some hours, then strain through a flannel jelly bag and cork down in the bottles. The best white vinegar should be used. In France the famous Vinegar of Maille is made in this way.

Tarragon vinegar is the only correct flavouring for Sauce Tartare, but must never be put into soups, as the taste is too strong and pungent. French cooks usually mix their mustard with Tarragon vinegar.

The Russian Tarragon is eaten in Persia to excite an appetite at meals.

Fresh Tarragon possesses an essential volatile oil, rather similar to that of Anise, which tends to become lost in the dried herb.

One pound of the oil is obtained by distilling 300 to 500lbs. of the green parts of the herb. It is used for perfuming toilet articles.

The root of Tarragon, held between the teeth, was said in the days of our forefathers to cure toothache, but one hears nothing of this use of it nowadays.

TARRAGON SAUCE

To a pint of good stock made from veal or poultry, add a small bunch of Tarragon, the white of egg whipped with a very little water and a tablespoonful of Tarragon Vinegar; continue whisking this over the fire until it boils, and then remove it to the side, there to remain boiling until the egg is thoroughly set hard and the aspic is perfectly bright; then strain it through a napkin into a stewpan and boil it down to the consistency of half glaze. This sauce or essence is used for "quenelles" and boiled fowls.

EGGS IN PASTRY

Roll out any pastry trimmings, cut into rounds and bake in patty pans. Chop parsley and Tarragon: make a thick white sauce. Poach some eggs. Turn the pastry cases out of the tins and place an egg in each case. Put the herbs into the sauce separately.

THYME
(N.O. LABIATÆ)

THYMUS VULGARIS Linn.
Local Name: Garden Thyme.

USES

THE WHOLE HERB for culinary purposes, flavouring, distilled as oil.

The Garden Thyme (*Thymus vulgaris*) the little aromatic sweet herb so familiar for its culinary use in stuffings, flavourings, etc., is an "improved" cultivated form of the

Wild Thyme of the mountains of Spain and other European countries bordering on the Mediterranean, flourishing also in Asia Minor, Algeria and Tunis, and is a near relation to our own Wild Thyme, *Thymus Serpyllum,* which, however, has broader leaves (the margins not reflexed as in the Garden Thyme) and also a weaker odour.

It is cultivated now in most countries with temperate climates, though it does not seem to have had any reputation in antiquity as a culinary herb, nor do we know at what period it was first introduced into northern countries, but for many centuries it has held an important place in the English kitchen-garden, especially before the introduction of Oriental spices, when, with other aromatic herbs, it was even more used in cookery than now. It was certainly commonly cultivated in England before the middle of the sixteenth century: how long previous to that is not known, but it was well figured and described by Gerarde.

The name Thyme, in its Greek form, was first given to the plant by the Greeks as a derivative from a word which meant "to fumigate," either because they used it as their incense, for its balsamic odour, or because it was taken as a type of all such sweet-smelling herbs. The antiseptic properties of Thyme were fully recognised in classic times, there being a reference in Virgil's *Georgics* to its use as a fumigator, and Pliny tells us that when burnt, it puts to flight all venomous creatures. Another theory as to the derivation of the name is that it comes from the Greek word *thumus,* signifying courage, the plant being held in ancient and mediæval times to be a great source of invigoration, its cordial qualities inspiring courage. It was, besides, an emblem of activity, bravery and energy, and in the days of chivalry, it was the custom for ladies to embroider the device of a bee hovering over a sprig of Thyme on the scarves they presented to their knights. In the south of France, Wild Thyme is a symbol of extreme Republicanism, tufts of it being sent with the summons to a meeting to members of a society holding those views.

Strangely enough, this little plant, so familiar also in its wild form, has never been known in this country by any other common native name, though occasionally "Thyme" is qualified in some way, such as "Running Thyme," or "Mother-of-Thyme." The latter name was probably originally "Mother Thyme," from its use in uterine disorders, in the same way that "Motherwort" (*Leonurus Cardiaca*) has received its popular name for similar use in the domestic medicine of the countryside.

The affection of bees for Thyme is well known, and the fine flavour of the honey of Mount Hymettus, near Athens, was said to be due to the Wild Thyme with which it was covered (probably *Thymus vulgaris*), the honey from this spot being of such especial flavour and sweetness that in the minds and writings of the ancients, sweetness and Thyme were indissolubly united. "Thyme, for the time it lasteth, yielded most and best honie and therefor in old time was accounted chief," says an old English writer. Large clumps of either Garden or Wild Thyme may with advantage be grown in the garden about 10ft. away from the hives.

Though apparently not in general use as a culinary herb among the ancients as it is now, it was employed by the Romans to give its peculiar aromatic flavour to cheese, a practice followed likewise, in modern days, not only with the leaves (see Sage pamphlet) but also with the flowers and seeds of other plants. The mountaineers in the Canton of Glaris, in Switzerland, prepare a cheese, known as *Schabzieger,* which is readily distinguished by its peculiar marbled appearance and aromatic flavour: these are communicated by the pressed flowers or the bruised seeds of the *Melilotus officinalis,* Common Melilot, which has a sweet, haylike scent.

DESCRIPTION. *Thymus vulgaris* is a perennial with a woody, fibrous root. The stems are numerous and are round, hard, branched and usually from 4 to 8ins. high, when of the largest growth scarcely attaining a foot in height. The leaves are small, only about 1/8in. long and 1/16in. broad, narrow and elliptical, greenish-grey in colour, reflexed at the margins, and set in pairs upon very small foot-stalks. The flowers terminate the branches in whorls. The calyx is tubular, striated, closed at the mouth with small hairs and divided into two lips, the uppermost cut into three teeth and the lower into two. The corolla consists of a tube about the length of the calyx, spreading at the top into two lips of a pale purple colour, the upper lip erect or turned back and notched at the end, the under lip longer and divided into three segments. The seeds are roundish and very small, about 170,000 to the ounce, it has been calculated, and 24ozs. to the quart: they retain their germinating power for three years. The plant has an agreeable aromatic smell and a warm pungent taste. The fragrance of its leaves is due to an essential oil, which gives it its flavouring value for culinary purposes, and is also the source of its medicinal properties. It is in flower from May to August.

Stocks may also be increased by dividing old roots, or making cuttings, by slipping pieces off the plants with roots to them and planting out with trowel or dibber, taking care to water well. This may be done as soon as the weather is warm enough, from May to September. The old clumps may be divided to the utmost extent, and provided each portion has a reasonable bit of root attached, success is assured. The perfume of Lemon Thyme is sweeter if raised from cuttings or division of roots, rather than from seed.

Although Thyme grows easily, especially in calcareous light, dry, stony soils, it can be cultivated in heavy soils, where, however, it is less aromatic. It dislikes excess of moisture. To form Thyme beds, choose uncultivated ground, with soil too poor to nourish cereals. If Thyme grows upon walls or on dry, stony land, it will survive the severest cold of this country. If the soil does not suit it very well, and is close and heavy, some material for lightening it, such as a little road sand or sweepings, ensuring reasonable porosity, will be welcomed and should be thoroughly incorporated; in a gritty soil it will root quickly, but does not like a close, cold soil about its roots.

According to Gattefosse, the Thyme is "a faithful companion of the Lavender. It lives together with it in perfect sympathy and partakes alike of its good and its bad fortune." Generally speaking, the conditions most suitable to the growth of Thyme are identical with those favoured by Lavender.

The plant is often overrun by Dodder (*Cuscuta Epithymum*). If this happens, cut off the affected plants and burn them, or use a solution of sulphate of iron.

At the close of the summer, as soon as the herbs have been cut as much as necessary, the beds should be attended to, all weeds cleared away and the soil well forked on the surface.

In winter, protect the plants from frost by banking up with earth.

Thyme roots greatly in the ground and soon extracts the goodness of the soil, hence whatever is sown or planted upon a spot of ground whereon Thyme grew in the preceding year, will seldom thrive unless the ground be first trenched deeper than the Thyme was rooted, and well manured.

The whole herb is used, fresh and dried. Though cultivated in gardens for culinary use, Common Thyme is not grown in England on a large scale, most of the dried Thyme on the market having been imported from the Continent, mainly from Germany.

Its essential oil is distilled in the south of France, the flowering herb being used for the production of Oil of Thyme. In the neighbourhood of Nîmes, the entire plant is used, and the distillation carried on at two periods of the year, in May and June, when the plant is first in flower, and again later in the autumn. In this country, only a comparatively small amount of the essential oil is distilled, but it is considered to be of a high quality.

The *fresh* herb for distilling should be collected on a dry day, when just coming into flower; the lower portions of the stem, together with any yellow or brown leaves, should be rejected and the herbs conveyed to the distillery as soon as possible. If necessary to travel by train, they may be packed in open crates—banana crates will do for the purpose—or light boxes, if possible, in quantities sufficient to fill a cattle truck, arranging for them to travel at night, for the sake of coolness (in which case they should be cut in the late afternoon) and labelling "Medicinal Plants, for immediate delivery. Urgent."

For *drying* (mainly for culinary purposes) tie up by the stalk ends in uniform-sized bunches, about a dozen in a bunch, and about 6ins. long. In this country Thyme is principally in request for culinary requirements, for its use, either fresh or dried, or in decoction, in flavouring stuffings, sauces, pickles, stews, soups, jugged hare, etc. The Spaniards infuse it in the pickle with which they preserve their olives.

The dried flowers have been often used in the same way as lavender, to preserve linen from insects.

All the different species of Thyme and Marjoram yield fragrant oils, extensively used by manufacturing perfumers for scenting soaps. When dried and ground, they enter into the composition of sachet powders.

Two commercial varieties of Thyme Oil are recognised, the "red," the crude distillate, and the "white" or colourless, which is the "red" when properly rectified by re-distilling. The yield of oil is very variable, from as low as ½ per cent. to 1 per cent. in the fresh herb (100lbs. of the fresh flowering tops yielding from ½ to 1lb. of essential oil) and 2.5 per cent. in the dried herb.

French Oil of Thyme is the most esteemed variety of the oil known. A considerable quantity of Thyme Oil is also distilled in Spain. A somewhat different oil is obtained from the Lemon Thyme, *Thymus Serpyllum* var. *citriodorus*. This oil has an odour resembling Thyme, Lemon and Geranium.

The Oil of Thyme obtained by distilling the fresh-flowering herb of *Thymus vulgaris* is already an article of commerce.

WILD THYME

(N.O. Labiatæ)

Thymus Serpyllum Linn.
    Local Name: Wild Thyme.

USES

Whole Herb for extraction of oil; used to flavour jugged hare, etc.

The Wild Thyme, *Thymus Serpyllum* Linn., is indigenous to the greater part of the dry land of Europe, though a great deal less abundant than the Common Thyme so widely cultivated. It is found up to a certain height on the Alps, on high plateaux, and in valleys, along ditches and roads, on rocks, in barren and dry soils, and also in damp clay soil destitute of chalk. It is seen in old stony, abandoned fields, dried-up lawns and on clearings. In this country it is found chiefly on heaths and in mountainous situations, and is also often cultivated as a border in gardens or on rockeries and sunny banks. It was a great favourite of Francis Bacon, who in giving us his plan for the perfect garden, directs that alleys should be planted with fragrant flowers: "burnet, wild thyme and watermints, which perfume the air most delightfully, being trodden upon and crushed," so that you may "have pleasure when you walk or tread."

The herb, wherever it grows wild, denotes a pure atmosphere and was thought to enliven the spirits by the fragrance which it diffuses into the air around. The Romans gave Thyme as a sovereign remedy to melancholy persons.

Wild Thyme is a perennial, more thickset than the Garden Thyme, though subject to many varieties, according to the surroundings in which it grows. In its most natural state, when found on dry exposed downs, it is small and procumbent, often forming dense cushions; when growing among furze or other plants which afford it shelter, it runs up a slender stalk to a foot or more in height, which gives it a totally different appearance. The specific name *Serpyllum* is derived from a Greek word meaning to creep, and has been given it from its usually procumbent and trailing habit.

The root is woody and fibrous, the stems numerous, hard,

branched, procumbent, rising from 4ins. to 1ft. high, ordinarily reddish-brown in colour. The bright green oval leaves, 1/8in. broad, tapering below into very short footstalks, are smooth and beset with numerous small glands. They are fringed with hairs towards the base and have the veins prominent on the under surfaces. Their margins are entire and not recurved as in Garden Thyme. As with all other members of the important order *Labiatæ,* to which the Thymes belong, the leaves are set in pairs on the stem. The plant flowers from the end of May or early June to the beginning of autumn, the flowers, which are very similar to those of the Garden Thyme, being purplish and in whorls at the top of the stems.

Bees, as already mentioned, are specially fond of the Thyme blossoms, from which they extract much honey. Spenser speaks of the "bees-alluring time," and everyone is familiar with Shakespeare's description of the "bank where the wild Thyme blows," the abode of the queen of the Fairies. It was looked upon as one of the fairies' flowers, tufts of Thyme forming one of their favourite playgrounds.

Thyme has somewhat strangely been associated with death; not only is it one of the fragrant flowers favoured in some parts for planting on graves (in Wales, particularly, none but sweet-scented plants being tolerated for this purpose), but the Order of Oddfellows to this day still carry sprigs of Thyme at funerals and throw them into the grave of their dead brother. An old tradition says that Thyme was one of the herbs that formed the fragrant bed of the Virgin Mary.

CULTIVATION. Wild Thyme will grow on any soil, but prefers light, sandy or gravelly ground exposed to the sun. Propagate by seeds, cuttings, or division of roots. Care must be taken to weed. Manure with farmyard manure in autumn or winter and nitrates in spring.

The whole herb is used. Cut when in full flower, in July and August, and dry in the same manner as for Common Thyme. It is much picked for sale in France, chiefly in the fields of the Aisne, for the extraction of its essential oil, a yellow liquid, with a weaker scent than that of Oil of Thyme, extracted from *Thymus vulgaris* and is called Oil of Serpolet. The flowering tops are used to flavour jugged hare, etc.; they have a milder and more grateful flavour than the Common Thyme. Although it has been stated that animals will seldom eat this plant and that rabbits do not touch it, yet according to others, it has been alleged that sheep love to crop its fragrant leaves and that, as a consequence, a fine flavour is then imparted to their flesh.

It is said that Wild Thyme and Marjoram laid by milk in the dairy will prevent it being turned by thunder.

WALNUT

(N.O. JUGLANDACEÆ)

JUGLANS REGIA Linn.
    Local Name: Walnut.

USES

NUT as nourishing food and to produce oil.
HUSKS AND LEAVES macerated in water to destroy garden worms; the juice made into a dark stain for floors, etc. Green husks for making dye.

Though the Walnut Tree will hardly be looked on as a culinary herb, yet its fruits may be included among those used for cookery, both as pickles and for the catsup prepared from them, which is used to flavour certain dishes.

The fruit, when young and unripe, makes a wholesome, anti-scorbutic pickle, slightly laxative.

WALNUT CATSUP

200 young green walnuts
4 quarts of vinegar
1lb. chopped shallots
4 cloves of garlic
4ozs. anchovies
½lb. of salt
4ozs. of whole peppers
1oz. cloves
½oz. of mace

Wash, then pound the Walnuts until well bruised. Put them into an unglazed jar with shallots, garlic, salt and vinegar and stir daily for ten days. Strain and put the liquor into a pan with the cloves, mace, pepper, and anchovies, and simmer for 20 minutes. Strain and pour into bottles. Cork well.

PICKLED WALNUTS

Walnuts for pickling should be gathered the first or second week in July, when they can be pierced with a pin easily, for when the shell hardens, and offers any resistance to the pin, they are too ripe to be pickled.

Make enough brine to cover them thoroughly, using 6ozs. of salt to the quart of water, carefully removing all the scum that rises as the salt dissolves, before you lay in the nuts. Stir them night and morning and change the brine every three days. After *nine* days in the brine, strain off the Walnuts and leave them on dishes exposed to the air until they turn quite black, which they will do in about 12 hours.

Now boil the vinegar, allowing half a gallon of vinegar to each 100 Walnuts, with (for each half gallon) a teaspoonful of salt, 2ozs. of black pepper, 3ozs. bruised ginger, a drachm of mace and ½oz. of cloves, stuck in two or three small onions, and 4ozs. of mustard seed. When these have been well boiled together for five minutes, pack the nuts in a deep stone jar and pour the vinegar, etc., over them hot from the fire. When quite cold, cover down closely and keep in a dry place. The Walnuts should always be covered with the vinegar, added fresh when needed, but being always careful to boil it before adding it to the pickle.

PART II

HERB BEERS, WINES, LIQUEURS, AND TEAS

PART II

HERB BEERS

FORMERLY every farmhouse inn had a brewing plant and brew-house attached to the buildings, and all brewed their own beer till the large breweries were established and supplanted home-brewed beers. Many of these farmhouses then began to brew their own "stingo" from wayside herbs, employing old rustic recipes that had been carried down from generation to generation. The true value of vegetable bitters and of herb beers has yet to be recognised by all sections of the community. Workmen in puddling furnaces and potteries in the Midland and Northern counties find, however, that a tea made of tonic herbs is cheaper and less intoxicating than ordinary beer and patronise the herb beers freely, *Dandelion Stout* ranking as one of the favourites. It is also made in Canada.

The following are recipes for Herb Beers collected from various sources.

BOTANIC BEER

2 ozs. meadowsweet
2 ozs. betony
2 ozs. agrimony
2 ozs. raspberry leaves
2½ lbs. white sugar
3 galls. water

DIRECTIONS. Boil the meadowsweet, betony, agrimony, and raspberry leaves in 3 galls. of water for a quarter of an hour; then strain and add the white sugar. When nearly cool, bottle. This beer does not require barm or yeast, but it can be improved by adding a little hyssop, 1 oz.

BURDOCK ALE

5 ozs.	burdock root
2 ozs.	camomile herb
4 ozs.	ginger
2½ lbs.	sugar
35 grns.	saccharine 550
2 ozs.	(or a sufficiency) foam essence
2 ozs.	burnt sugar
10 galls.	water

DIRECTIONS. Boil the burdock, camomile, and ginger in half the water for 15 minutes; add the burnt sugar and pour through a strainer on to the sugar and saccharine. Stir until it is all dissolved, then add the remainder of the water and foam essence. Add a sufficient quantity of yeast, allow to work for 12 hours at a temperature of 65° to 70°F. Skim off the yeast and bottle for use.

BURDOCK AND DANDELION ALE

2½ ozs.	burdock leaves
2½ ozs.	dandelion leaves
2 ozs.	block juice
35 grns.	saccharine 550
2½ lbs.	sugar
10 galls.	water
2 ozs.	(or a sufficiency) burnt sugar
2 ozs.	foam essence

Directions. Boil the burdock, dandelion, and block juice in half the quantity of water for 15 minutes; add the burnt sugar and pour through a strainer on to the sugar and saccharine. Stir until dissolved, then add the remainder of the water and foam essence. Add a sufficient quantity of yeast, allow to work for 12 hours at a temperature of 65° to 70°F. Skim off the yeast and bottle for use.

CAMOMILE BEER

'12 ozs.	camomile herb (English)
4 ozs.	ground ginger
4 ozs.	cream of tartar
35 grns.	saccharine 550
2½ lbs.	sugar
2 ozs.	burnt sugar
10 galls.	water

Directions. Infuse the camomile herb and ginger in 5 galls. of boiling water for 15 minutes in a covered vessel. Strain and pour on to the sugar and saccharine, and stir until dissolved. Then add the burnt sugar, cream of tartar, and 5 galls. of cold water. Mix well, add the yeast, and ferment in the usual way.

DANDELION BEER

2 ozs.	dried dandelion herb
2 ozs.	dried nettle herb
1 oz.	yellow dock
2 lbs.	sugar
2 tablespoonfuls	ground ginger

Directions. Take the dandelion and nettle herbs, and the yellow dock and boil in 1 gall. of water for 15 minutes, and then strain the liquor while hot on to the 2 lbs. of sugar, on the top of which is sprinkled the ground ginger. Leave until milk-warm, then add boiled water gone cold to bring the quantity up to 2 galls. The temperature must not then be above 75°F. Now dissolve ½oz. of solid yeast in a little of the liquid and stir into the bulk. Allow to ferment for 24 hours, skim and bottle, and it will be ready for use in a day or two.

DANDELION STOUT

1 oz.	balm
5 ozs.	dandelion herb
5 ozs.	ground ginger
2 ozs.	block juice
35 grns.	saccharine 550
2½ lbs.	sugar
10 galls.	water

DIRECTIONS. Boil the ingredients in half the amount of water for 15 minutes, then pour through a strainer on to the sugar and saccharine. Stir until dissolved, then add the remainder of the water. Add a sufficient quantity of yeast and allow it to work for 12 hours at a temperature of from 65° to 70°F. Skim off the yeast and bottle for use.

HOP ALE

1 oz.	hops
½ oz.	bruised ginger root
1½ lbs.	Demerara sugar
3 pts.	water

DIRECTIONS. Home-made Hop Ale is a very simple process and is supposed to keep for at least a week. Take 1 oz. of hops and the bruised ginger and put it in 3 pts. of water, boiling it for half an hour. Then add the sugar and reboil until all the sugar is dissolved. Pour the liquid into an earthenware pan and allow to stand overnight. Next day draw it off gradually into another vessel, and bottle.

HOREHOUND BEER

DIRECTIONS. Take a handful of Horehound and put in 3 galls. of water with two pounds of treacle. Boil for an hour, then strain and cool to the temperature of new milk. Then add two tablespoonfuls of yeast and let it stand for 24 hours. After then it is ready to be bottled.

ANOTHER RECIPE FOR HOREHOUND BEER

1 lb.	horehound
4 ozs.	ginger
2 ozs.	block juice
2 ozs.	coriander seed
2 ozs.	foam essence
35 grns.	saccharine 550
2½ lbs.	sugar
10 galls.	water

DIRECTIONS. Boil the Horehound, ginger, and coriander seeds in half the water for 15 minutes; add the block juice, and stir until dissolved; strain and pour on to the sugar and saccharine. Stir well, and then add the foam essence and ferment.

A HOREHOUND DRINK

3 sprays	horehound
1½ oz.	hops
1 oz.	whole ginger (bruised)
1½ ozs.	sugar
1½ galls.	water

DIRECTIONS. Boil for an hour and strain. When lukewarm put in a little yeast. After 12 hours, bottle and cork. This is then ready to drink.

A HERB BEER

2 drms.	extract of hops
4 „	„ camomile
4 „	„ gentian
5 ozs.	ground ginger
2½ lbs.	sugar
2 ozs.	foam essence
35 grns.	saccharine 550
10 galls.	water
2 ozs.	burnt sugar

DIRECTIONS. Boil the Ginger in half the water for 20 minutes, and dissolve the extracts in the hot liquor. Strain and run on to the Sugar and Saccharine. Stir till dissolved. Add other ingredients and ferment in the usual way.

ROOT BEER

1 quart	Sorrel Leaves
1 pint	Horehound Leaves
1¼ pints	Dandelion Roots
4	Lemons
½ pint	Red and Black Currants
1 oz.	Whole Ginger
2 lbs.	Brown Sugar
1 gall.	Water

DIRECTIONS. Take the Sorrel leaves, Horehound leaves, and Dandelion roots and wash them thoroughly; put into a saucepan, add four sliced Lemons, the Red and Black Currants, Ginger, Sugar, and the gallon of water. Boil very gently for an hour and a half, strain, and when lukewarm add a teaspoonful of cream of tartar and one yeast cake dissolved in a little lukewarm water. Cover and stand in a warm place for three days, then skim, bottle and seal. In a fortnight it will be ready for use.

MEADOWSWEET DRINK

Meadowsweet mash, worked with barm and a little sugar, makes a very good drink.

NETTLE BEER

2 Lemons and some fresh Nettle tops
1 teaspoonful of Ground Ginger
1 lb. Brown Sugar
1 gall. water

DIRECTIONS. Take a quantity of young, fresh Nettle tops and boil in 1 gallon of water, with the juice of the two lemons, crushed ginger, and sugar. Fresh yeast is floated on toast in the liquor, when cold, to ferment it, and when it is bottled, the result is a specially wholesome sort of ginger-beer.

NETTLE BEER
(Another Recipe)

1 peck Nettles
1 oz. Bruised Ginger
1 lb. Lump Sugar
1 Lemon

DIRECTIONS. Wash the Nettles well, and, adding the bruised ginger, cover them with water and boil for half an hour. Whilst they are boiling, take a large earthenware bowl and put in it the lump sugar and the lemon cut into thin slices; then, placing a strainer across, pour over it the contents of the pan. This ought to make one gallon of the liquid, but if there should not be enough, add a little more water to the Nettles and reboil before making up the required quantity. Toast a slice of bread and put it in the bowl and add a breakfastcupful of barm as soon as it is lukewarm, not before, or you will scald the barm and prevent it working. When you have put in the barm, stir it all thoroughly and leave the bowl covered on the hearth to work for eight hours and then skim off the barm, and bottle. It is very much improved by the addition of some Dandelion roots.

HERB WINES

The following Recipes are given as a guide to making Herb Wines at home.

BALM WINE

DIRECTIONS. Put 10 lbs. of moist sugar into 4 gallons of water and boil for over an hour, skimming thoroughly. Then pour it into a vessel to cool. Take 1¼ lbs. of Balm tops (bruised) and place in a small cask with a little fresh yeast, and when the liquor is cool pour it over the Balm. Stir it up well and let the mixture stand for 24 hours, stirring it at frequent intervals. Then close it up, lightly at first, and more securely after fermentation has quite ceased. When it has been standing for six or eight weeks, bottle it, putting a piece of lump sugar into each bottle. Cork the bottles firmly and keep for at least a year before using it.

BRAMBLE-TIP WINE

DIRECTIONS. The green shoots should be gathered in May or the beginning of June, whilst they are still tender, and a gallon of the tips should be boiled for 1 hour in a gallon of water, together with 4 lbs. of Demerara sugar. The liquid should then be strained and allowed to ferment, after which it should be bottled. It will be ready for use in 12 months.

COLTSFOOT WINE

> 2 qts. Coltsfoot flowers
> 1 gallon of water
> 3 lbs. sugar
> 1 tea-cupful of raisins to 4 gallons
> 3 Seville Oranges
> 2 Lemons

DIRECTIONS. The flowers should be measured when freshly gathered, then spread out on trays to dry. When quite dry put them into a pan and pour the boiling water on them and let them stand for three days, stirring three times each day. Then strain off the liquor, add the sugar, and boil well for half an hour. When cold put some yeast on a piece of toast into the liquid and let it ferment. Next day, remove the toast, put the liquor into a cask and add the raisins, oranges, and lemons, cut up. Let it stand for three months, and then it will be ready to bottle.

COMFREY WINE

> 4 lbs. Comfrey root (weighed after being cut up)
> 1 gall. water
> 3 lbs. Sugar to each gallon.

DIRECTIONS. Clean, peel, and cut up the roots into pieces about 4 or 5 inches long. Boil until quite tender, and then remove the lid to allow the strong smell to escape. Strain off the liquid, and to every gallon allow 3 lbs. of sugar. Boil these together for ¾ hour, then pour the liquor into a pan, and when tepid add a very little yeast on toast. Let it stand for at least 10 days covered over, and stir it every day. Then put it into a cask or stone jar to work. In six or seven months the wine will be ready to bottle.

THREE RECIPES FOR COWSLIP WINE

DIRECTIONS. No. 1. To 5 quarts of water add 2lbs. of sugar and make a syrup. Pour this, whilst it is hot, over a quart of cowslips (just the yellow flower part). Let it stand for 24 hours. Strain, add 2 tablespoonfuls of yeast spread upon a piece of toast, and leave standing for 10 days, stirring at least once every day for the first 4 days. When the 10 days are up, strain and bottle.

DIRECTIONS. No. 2. Allow 3lbs. of sugar, 2 lemons, and 1 gallon of cowslips (when the flowers have been separated from the stalks and seeds) to 1 gallon of water. Boil the sugar and water together, and when this has cooled to milk heat, pour over the cowslips and lemon-peel. Ferment with fresh brewer's barm spread on a slice of toast, allowing 1 tablespoonful of barm to 3 gallons of liquor.

DIRECTIONS. No. 3. To 2 gallons of water allow 2½lbs. of sugar, 2 lemons, and 4 quarts of cowslip flowers. Put the water and sugar into a preserving-pan, bring it to the boil, and boil for half an hour, carefully removing any scum that rises. Then pour this liquid into a tub over the thinly peeled rind of the lemons and leave it to cool. When cold add the strained juice of the lemons and the cowslip flowers, using only the tops. Cover and leave the mixture to stand for 2 days, stirring well every two or three hours. Put into a barrel and let it stand three weeks or a month. When bottling place a lump of sugar into each bottle.

SIX RECIPES FOR DANDELION WINE

DIRECTIONS. No. 1. To every gallon of freshly gathered flowers, allow 1 gallon of water, half a lemon rind to every gallon of liquor, 1 lb. of sugar to every quart, and 1 tablespoonful of yeast. Pour the boiling water on the flowers and lemon-peel. Let it stand for 14 days. Then strain off the liquor, add the sugar and a piece of toast with the yeast on it, and let it ferment. Keep the cask filled up with added water whilst it is working. When it has finished working, bottle it. Cork the bottles tightly and keep in a cool place. This wine may be made of half Dandelions and half Cowslips.

DIRECTIONS. No. 2. To every quart of blossoms allow:—

    1 quart of water
    a little ginger root
    3 Cloves
    5 Chillies

Boil all the ingredients for half an hour and then strain. Allow 5½lbs. of sugar to every 6 quarts of liquid, add the rind of a lemon and the juice, strained, then boil it all up again for half an hour. When lukewarm, place yeast in it spread on a piece of toasted bread. Put the liquid into a stone vessel and let it ferment for 14 days, then pour into a stone jar or bottles, and cork up. It will be ready for use in 6 months' time.

DIRECTIONS. No. 3. Put 4 quarts of Dandelion blossoms, without stems, into a tub. Pour over them one gallon of cold water. Cover the tub with a thick cloth or sack, and let it stand 3 days, keeping it well stirred at intervals during the time. Then strain off the liquor, and boil it for half an hour with the addition of 3½lbs. of loaf sugar, a little ginger sliced, the rind of one orange, and one lemon sliced; let it cool, then ferment with a little yeast on toast. Cover it over and let it stand 2 days, until it has ceased to work. Then pour it into a cask, and put in the bung, but not too tightly, for a week or two. Leave it thus well bunged down for two months before bottling. The wine suggests sherry slightly flat.

DIRECTIONS. No. 4. This is made by pouring a gallon of boiling water over a gallon of flowers. After being well stirred, it is covered with a blanket and stirred again at intervals, after which it is strained and the liquor boiled for 30 minutes, with the addition of ginger, lump sugar and lemon- or orange-peel. When cold a little yeast is placed in it on a piece of toast, producing fermentation. After a couple of days it is placed in a cask and bottled in 2 months' time.

DIRECTIONS. No. 5.

2 quarts Dandelion flowers
1 gallon water
Juice and rind of two oranges
Juice and rind of one lemon
2 tablespoonfuls of yeast
3lbs. loaf sugar.

Put the flowers in the water and bring to the boil; then add the rind of oranges and lemon and the sugar and boil for an hour. Strain and, when nearly cold, add the yeast, bottle the next day, adding juice of oranges and lemon, also a few raisins. Do not cork down until it has done working, which will be in about three weeks.

DIRECTIONS. No. 6. A recipe by Mrs. Legg.

Gather a gallon of Dandelion Flowers on a dry day. Put them into a large bowl, and cover them with a gallon of boiling water. Cover over with a cloth and leave for three days, stirring well from time to time. Then strain off into a preserving-pan, add the thinly-pared and finely-chopped rind of one orange and one lemon, 3lbs. of lump sugar, and a small piece of ginger.

Strip the white pith off the lemon, quarter it, remove the pips and add the remainder of the fruit, broken in small pieces. Simmer gently for half an hour, turn into a dry pan, leave to cool, spread a tablespoonful of yeast on a piece of dry toast, add and allow to work for two days. Strain into a dry cask, bung down closely and rack off in bottles in about 10 weeks' time.

SOME ELDER WINE RECIPES

An old cookery-book recipe for Elder Wine.

"To every quart of berries put 2 quarts of water; boil half an hour, run the liquor and break the fruit through a hair-sieve; then to every quart of juice, put ¾lb. of Lisbon sugar, coarse, but not the very coarsest. Boil the whole a quarter of an hour with some Jamaica peppers, ginger, and a few cloves. Pour it into a tub, and when of a proper warmth, into the barrel with toast and yeast to work, which there is more difficulty to make it do than most other liquors. When it ceases to hiss, put a quart of brandy to eight gallons and stop up. Bottle in the spring, or at Christmas. The liquor must be in a warm place to make it work."

The following recipe for making Elder Wine is given by Mrs. Hewlett, in a work entitled *Cottage Comforts.*

"If two gallons of wine are to be made, get one gallon of elder-berries and a quart of damsons, or sloes; boil them together in six quarts of water for half an hour, breaking the fruit with a stick, flat at one end; run off the liquor, and squeeze the pulp through a sieve, or straining-cloth; boil the liquor up again with six pounds of coarse sugar, two ounces of ginger, two ounces of bruised allspice, and one ounce of hops (the spice had better be loosely tied in a bit of muslin); let this boil above half an hour; then pour it off; when quite cool, stir in a tea-cupful of yeast, and cover it up to work. After two days, skim off the yeast, and put the wine into the barrel, and when it ceases to hiss, which will be in about a fortnight, paste a stiff brown paper over the bung-hole. After this, it will be fit for use in about eight weeks, but will keep eight years if required. The bag of spice may be dropped in at the bung-hole, having a string fastened outside, which shall keep it from reaching the bottom of the barrel."

ANOTHER RECIPE

"Strip the berries, which must be quite ripe, into a dry pan and pour 2 gallons of boiling water over 3 gallons of berries. Cover and leave in a warm place for 24 hours; then strain, pressing the juice well out. Measure it and allow 3lbs. of sugar, ½oz. of ginger and ¼oz. of cloves to each gallon. Boil for 20 minutes slowly, then strain it into a cask and ferment when lukewarm. Let it remain until still before bunging, and bottle in six months.

"If a weaker wine is preferred, use 4 gallons of water to 3 gallons of berries and leave for two days before straining.

"If a cask be not available, large stone jars will answer: then the wine need not be bottled."

Parkinson tells us that fresh Elder Flowers hung in a vessel of new wine and pressed every evening for seven nights together, "giveth to the wine a very good relish and a smell like Muscadine." Ale was also infused with Elder flowers.

MEAD

1 blade of mace
6 qts. of water
2½lbs. of honey
½ teaspoonful powdered cinnamon
a little bruised ginger
2 cloves
2 eggs

Directions. Put the 6 quarts of water into a pan; add the honey, cinnamon, mace, ginger, cloves, and the beaten whites of the eggs. Heat, and whisk frequently, until the mixture comes to the boil, then simmer gently for an hour. When lukewarm strain into a cask and add a small tablespoonful of yeast, and cover the bung-hole with a folded cloth until fermentation stops. Bung the cask tightly, and bottle the Mead in nine months' time.

MULBERRY WINE

On each gallon of ripe Mulberries, pour one gallon of boiling water and let them stand for two days. Then squeeze all through a hair sieve or bag. Wash out the tub or jar and return the liquor to it, put in the sugar at the rate of 3lbs. to each gallon of the liquor; stir up until quite dissolved, then put the liquor into a cask. Let the cask be raised a little on one side until fermentation ceases, then bung down. If the liquor be clear, it may be bottled in four months' time. Into each bottle put one clove and a small lump of sugar and the bottles should be kept in a moderate temperature. The wine may be used in a year from time of bottling.

Mulberries are sometimes used in Devonshire for mixing with cider during fermentation, giving a pleasant taste and deep red colour. In Greece, also, the fruit is subjected to fermentation, thereby furnishing an inebriating beverage.

OAK-LEAF WINE

NOTE.—The shoots for this must be gathered very young, and 16lbs. of sugar are allowed to ten young oak leaves, 4 gallons of water, and four lemons. To this quantity allow 4ozs. of yeast.

DIRECTIONS. Put the oak leaves into a pan, pour the water over them and let them steep for eight hours. Then add the sugar and the lemons, cut into slices, and let the whole simmer for 20 minutes. Let it cool down, and then add the yeast when it is lukewarm. Let it stand for 36 hours, and it must be put into a cask after the fermentation has ceased. It should be ready for use in six to eight months.

PARSNIP WINE

DIRECTIONS. No. 1. To every 4lbs. of parsnips, cleaned and sliced thin, put a gallon of water, boil the parsnips until they are quite soft, and strain the liquor off without crushing the parsnips. To every gallon of the liquor put 3lbs. of loaf sugar and ½oz. of crude Tartar. When nearly cold add fresh yeast spread on a slice of toast, an ounce of yeast to four gallons of liquor. Cover and leave to ferment in a warm place for about seven days. Then strain into a cask or jar and bottle after three to six months.

DIRECTIONS. No. 2. Take 15lbs. of sliced parsnips and boil until soft in five gallons of water. Squeeze the liquor out of them, run through a sieve and add 3lbs. of lump sugar to every gallon. Boil for ¾ hour, and when nearly cold add a little yeast spread on toast. Let it remain in the tub for 10 days. Stir up from the bottom every day, then put it into a cask for a year. As it works over, fill it up every time.

DIRECTIONS. No. 3. Ingredients:—
    18lbs. parsnips
    2 tablespoonfuls of yeast to each 6 galls.
    10 gallons of water
    3lbs. loaf sugar to each gall.

Clean the parsnips, cut them into quarters, and then into pieces about 4ins. long. Put them into a large pan and add the water; bring to the boil, skim, cover the pan and boil until the parsnips are soft. Remove the lid from the pan and cool the contents slightly, then strain the liquid through a hair sieve into a clean tub. Measure, and add 3lbs. sugar to each gallon of the liquor and stir until the sugar has dissolved. When the wine is almost cold spread two tablespoonfuls of yeast to each six gallons of wine on a thick slice of toast, and add it to the liquid. Cover the tub with a piece of flannel and stir the mixture daily for ten days, and skim frequently. Put the wine into a clean cask and leave it for a day or two for fermentation to subside. Cover the bung-hole with a piece of brown paper, and if this remains intact for a day or two, bung the cask up tightly and keep it in a cool place with an even temperature of 50 to 55 degrees. This wine should be ready to bottle in six or seven months' time.

RHUBARB WINE

DIRECTIONS. No. 1. Chop the stalks of the rhubarb coarsely and to every quart add three quarts of water, and let it stand for two or three days; at the end of that time strain through a cloth, and to every quart add one pound of sugar. Let this remain in jars to ferment, skimming every day until fermentation ceases and then bottle.

DIRECTIONS. No. 2. Ingredients:—
    20 lbs. rhubarb
    5 galls. water—boiled and allowed to get cold
    12 lbs. lump sugar
    1 pt. French brandy
    ½ lb. barley sugar
    ½ oz. isinglass
    2 oranges
    2 lemons.

Wipe the rhubarb with a damp cloth and slice it thinly into an earthenware or clean wooden vessel; pour the water over it and allow it to stand, closely covered, for four days; strain it through a fine hair sieve or jelly-bag, pressing the pulp gently to extract all the juice, add the sugar, stirring occasionally till all is dissolved; then turn the preparation into a cask and cover the bung-hole with a folded cloth; as soon as the fermentation ceases, add the brandy, bung the cask closely and allow it to stand undisturbed for three months; rack the wine into a clean, dry cask, add the thinly-cut orange and lemon peel, and the barley sugar finely powdered, and the isinglass dissolved in warm water; bung the cask closely and allow it to stand in a cool, dry place for at least 12 months —the longer the better; then bottle, cork and seal securely, and store for six months at least after bottling.

ROSE WINE

DIRECTIONS. Put into a well-glazed earthen vessel three gallons of rose-water drawn with a cold still. Put into it a sufficient quantity of rose-leaves, cover it close, and set it for an hour in a kettle or copper of hot water, to take out all the strength and flavour of the roses. When it is cold, press the rose-leaves hard into the liquor, and steep fresh ones in it, repeating it until the liquor has got the full strength of the roses. To every gallon of liquor put 3lbs. of loaf sugar, and stir it well, that it may melt and disperse in every part. Then put it into a cask or other convenient vessel to ferment, and throw into it a piece of bread toasted hard and covered with yeast. Let it stand a month, when it will be ripe and have all the fine flavour and scent of the roses. If you add some wine and spices, it will be a considerable improvement.

ROSEMARY WINE

DIRECTIONS. Chop up sprigs of fresh green Rosemary and pour on them white wine and leave to steep for three or four days; then strain and bottle and it is ready for use.

VARIOUS HERB DRINKS

DIRECTIONS. No. 1. Meadowsweet, Yarrow, Dandelion, Nettle, and Honey, worked with yeast, and bottled, make a good drink.

DIRECTIONS. No. 2. Take 2ozs. each of Dandelion, Meadowsweet, and Agrimony, to 2 gallons of water; boil for 20 minutes, add 2lbs. of sugar, and ½ pint of yeast. Stand in a warm place for 12 hours, then bottle.

DIRECTIONS. No. 3. Boil a quart of water down to 2/3, add 20–30 leaves of Sage, half that amount of Rosemary, 15–20 grains of English Saffron. Infuse for ¼ hour, well covered, pour off and drink hot with sugar.

DIRECTIONS. No. 4. 1lb. each of Wormwood, Spearmint, and Balm. 2lbs. Holy Thistle. Distil with 2 gallons of milk.

HERB LIQUEURS

ANGELICA LIQUEUR

1 oz. Angelica stems
1 oz. Bitter Almonds
2 pints Brandy

DIRECTIONS. Take the freshly-gathered Angelica stems, and after chopping them up, steep them in 2 pints of good brandy for five days, 1 oz. of skinned and pulped Bitter Almonds being added. Then strain the liquid through muslin and add a pint of liquid sugar to it.

MARIGOLD CORDIAL

1 peck of Marigold petals
1½lbs. stoned raisins
7lbs. sugar
2lbs. honey
3 galls. water

DIRECTIONS. Gather Marigold petals daily, in July, until about a peck has been collected; add to them 1½lbs. of stoned raisins, and pour over them a boiling liquid made with the 7lbs. of sugar, 2lbs. honey, and 3 gallons of water. Clear the liquid first, whilst boiling, with the whites and shells of three eggs and strain before pouring over the flowers. Cover the vessel closely—use preferably a deep brown pipkin—and let it stand for 24 hours. Then stir, cover again, and leave until the third morning. Strain off the whole into a cask and to the liquor add the rinds (pared without the white) of oranges and a pound of sugar candy. Then put in four or five table-spoonfuls of good brewer's yeast and cover the bung-hole. Leave the wine to work until it froths out. When all fermentation has ceased, put in a pint of brandy and ½oz. of dissolved isinglass, and stop up the cask, leaving it untouched for some months.

PEPPERMINT CORDIAL

2 drachms Oil of Peppermint.
2 ounces Rectified Spirit
1 gallon Plain Syrup

DIRECTIONS. Dissolve the oil in the rectified spirit and mix with the syrup. Allow to stand for a few days and draw off from the bottom. Any excess of oil not taken up by the syrup floats to the top. So that it is advisable to retain the last half-pint or so of the cordial and mix with the next batch. Cinnamon, Clove, Aniseed, and other cordials are prepared in a similar manner and coloured with the addition of 4ozs. of Caramel to each gallon of cordial.

HERB TEAS

The study of herbs has been neglected—except by a few people—for many years, but now there are signs that it is being slowly revived. It is not at all an unusual thing to find a portion set aside for herbs in country gardens, cultivated by those who really understand something of their properties.

Many things which we dislike at first, we afterwards acquire a taste for, and there is no doubt that Herb Teas *are* an acquired taste. They have a strange smell and a strange flavour, and that is the reason why they are not popular, for many people do not try to get used to them. Yet if the taste for them is cultivated, they certainly improve on acquaintance.

The following few recipes are interesting.

APPETISING BITTERS

DIRECTIONS. Take equal parts of Germander, Centaury, and Blessed Thistle and infuse. An equal amount of Buckbean may also be added.

BALM TEA

> 12 Sprigs of young Balm
> 2 Teaspoonfuls of Sugar
> 6 Cloves
> The juice of half a Lemon

Directions. Pour the pint of boiling water on all the ingredients and steep in a covered jug for about an hour. Then strain the liquor through muslin and bottle it. It will keep for one or two days. Nettle sprigs may be used with the Balm. The flavour of this tea is like that of acid-drops—it is usually taken at bed-time for a cold.

CAMOMILE TEA

Directions. Take a teaspoonful of Camomile Flowers and wash them well to remove any dust, and place in a teapot; then pour into the pot about a pint of boiling water. Let it stand for three or four minutes before straining, and sweeten if required.

GROUND IVY OR "GILL" TEA

Directions. Take one ounce of the bruised fresh herb and infuse in a pint of boiling water, sweetening with honey, sugar, or liquorice.

HERB TEA. NO. I
(Substitute for Tea)
(From *The Family Handbook*)

> 5 ozs. Rose leaves, dried
> 1 oz. Rosemary
> 2 ozs. Balm

Directions. Mix well together, a dessertspoonful is sufficient for a half-pint of boiling water. Infuse for a few minutes and drink as tea, with sugar and milk as desired.

HERB TEA. NO. 2

DIRECTIONS. Take equal parts of Aniseed, Fennel, Caraway, and Coriander. Infuse by pouring on boiling water. Leave until cool, and strain, or drink hot if preferred.

HERB TEA. NO. 3

DIRECTIONS. Take equal parts of Sage, Rosemary, Thyme, Wild Thyme, Hyssop, Marjoram, Wormwood, and Peppermint. Infuse by pouring on boiling water. Leave until cool, and then strain, or drink hot, as preferred.

HERB TEA. NO. 4

Take:—

1	handful	Fennel roots
1	„	Parsley roots
½	„	Borage roots
½	„	Pennyroyal roots
½	„	Violet roots
½	„	Succory roots
½	„	Endive roots
½	„	Hollyhock leaves
½	„	Mallow leaves
½	„	Red Garden Mint leaves
½	„	Liquorice root (scraped, bruised, and powdered)
1½	gallons	Water

Add to this:—

> 3 spoonfuls Aniseed
> 3   „   Fennel Seed
> 3   „   Coriander Seed
> 3   „   Cumin Seed
> 1 handful Dandelion Root

DIRECTIONS. Put above into 1½ gallons water, boil to ¾ gall. down to clear point, strain and drink either warm or cold 3 wineglassfuls per day.

HERB TEA. NO. 5

> 1   handful Borage
> 1   „   Sorrel
> 1   „   Endive
> 1   „   Cinquefoil
> 2 or 3 handfuls Barley
> ½   handful Red Fennel roots

DIRECTIONS. Take the above-mentioned ingredients and put them into one gallon of water, adding liquorice, sugar, figs, dates, and raisins. Boil from one gallon down to three pints, and strain.

HERB TEA. NO. 6

Take equal parts of:—
> Aniseed
> Fennel
> Caraway
> Coriander

DIRECTIONS. Infuse by pouring on boiling water; leave until cool and strain or drink hot, as preferred.

HERB TEA. NO. 7

2 ozs. Meadowsweet
2 ozs. Agrimony
2 ozs. Betony
2 ozs. Raspberry
2 galls. Water

DIRECTIONS. Put the ingredients in a pan in the 2 gallons of water and boil for 15 minutes; then add 2lbs. of white sugar, and bottle.

HOP BITTERS

½ oz. Hops
1 oz. Angelica
1 oz. Holy Thistle.

DIRECTIONS. Pour 3 pints of boiling water on the above ingredients and strain when cold. A wineglassful may be taken four times a day as an appetiser.

PEPPERMINT TEA

DIRECTIONS. Take about a teaspoonful of the leaves and pour on them nearly a pint of boiling water; let the infusion draw from five to ten minutes, according to the strength you like. Strain, and it is then ready to drink.

SAGE TEA

DIRECTIONS. No. 1. Take half an ounce of fresh Sage leaves —without the stalks—and wash them clean in cold water; add one ounce of sugar, and the outer rind of a lemon, peeled very thinly. Put these ingredients into 2 pints of boiling water and put the mixture on the fire for half an hour. Then strain and it is ready for use. If dried Sage leaves are used instead of the fresh, do not use so many.

SAGE TEA

DIRECTIONS. No. 2. Take two tablespoonfuls of Sage leaves and pour on to them one pint of boiling water, just as you would make ordinary tea. Allow it to stand about five minutes before straining, then add a teaspoonful or more of orange juice to flavour it.

PART III
CONDIMENTS, ETC.

PART III

CONDIMENTS, ETC.

CONDIMENTS may be defined as flavouring materials which are added to food, more especially food of a savoury character, after it has been served at table. But the term is not a precise one, as all the flavouring materials used in this way are also employed for spicing food during the process of cooking. Moreover, salt is invariably included amongst condiments, and this material, though possessed of a very characteristic taste, is, correctly speaking, devoid of flavour. The other materials commonly used as condiments in England are mustard, pepper, and vinegar, the nature and uses of which will now be briefly described.

MUSTARD

MUSTARD is prepared from the seeds of certain plants belonging to the Natural Order *Cruciferæ,* or Cress Family, and closely related to the Cabbage. They are White Mustard, *Brassica alba* Boiss., Black Mustard, *Brassica nigra* Koch, and Indian Mustard or Rai, *Brassica juncea* Coss.

VARIETIES OF MUSTARD. Both White and Black Mustards can be found growing wild in Great Britain. The first is not truly native, but is perfectly naturalised. The plants somewhat resemble Charlock, from which, however, they may be distinguished by many features. Black Mustard has rather smaller flowers and is less hairy. Its seed-pods are smooth, four-angled, and pressed against the stems. White Mustard, on the other hand, has large flowers and produces hairy seed-pods. These are cylindrical in shape, short, but furnished with long beaks. They stand out well from the stems on rather long foot-stalks.

Both plants are exceedingly easy to grow on well-manured soil. White Mustard is cultivated in this country on a commercial scale for its seeds, but for supplies of the black variety, we are partly dependent on other countries, such as Holland and Italy.

It would be quite a simple matter for everyone with a garden to grow these two plants for their own use. Unfortunately, however, the quality of the condiment depends a great deal on the grinding, which cannot be economically effected on a small scale.

CHARACTERS AND COMPOSITION. The seeds of Black Mustard are very small and dark brown in colour. Those of White Mustard are yellowish and larger. Genuine Indian Mustard seed closely resembles Black Mustard seed, and is specially recommended for use in curries.

All varieties of mustard seeds contain fixed oil, proteins, and mucilage. From the point of view of their utility as condiments, however, the most important constituents are certain sugar-compounds or glucosides and a mixture of active substances or enzymes called "myrosin." The sugar-compound present in White Mustard seed is different from that in Black Mustard seed. In the presence of water, the myrosin in White Mustard seed acts on its peculiar sugar-compound, producing, amongst other substances, a sulphur-compound of very pungent taste. This substance is practically non-volatile, hence it is devoid of aroma.

In the case of Black Mustard seed, treatment with water induces somewhat similar chemical changes, a different sulphur-compound, however, being produced. This substance has not only a very pungent taste, but it is volatile and has a very powerful odour. It is the chief constituent of the volatile oil of mustard.

This oil is, physiologically speaking, very powerful. Its odour is quite unbearable, and, applied to the skin, the oil rapidly produces blisters. Nevertheless, when present only in traces, its odour becomes agreeably aromatic and its flavour is equally pleasant.

PREPARED MUSTARD. These facts explain why, when we wish to use mustard as a condiment, we always first prepare it by mixing the mustard with water, vinegar, or milk. This preliminary treatment is necessary to bring about the changes mentioned above, so that the pungency of the mustard may be at once evident on tasting it. It is very important never to use hot water for this purpose. Cold water, or, if preferred, cold vinegar or milk, should be used; otherwise the heat will adversely affect the myrosin and the mustard will, in consequence, lack flavour.

On the Continent it is customary to purchase mustard in a form ready for use at table. This is manufactured by mixing ground mustard with vinegar, salt, and sometimes other flavouring materials, the exact composition of the pastes often being closely guarded trade secrets.

In England it is more usual to buy mustard in the form of a fine powder or flour ready for mixing with water. It is said that the idea of grinding mustard seeds and sifting the resulting flour originated with a clever Englishwoman (Mrs. Clements, of Durham) in the early part of the eighteenth century.

The best results are thought to be got by using a mixture of the black and white mustards, hence the term "double mustard." Indian mustard is also employed. Fine grinding is essential for a good product. Frequently, part of the fixed oil is removed by hydraulic pressure, and the husks are usually removed by winnowing, as they hinder efficient grinding.

Various more or less worthless additions are commonly made to the resulting flour, which is then sold under some such fancy name as "mustard condiment." These include seeds of worthless *Brassica* species, turmeric (to brighten the colour), and cornflour. Although the adulterants mentioned are harmless, the housewife will do well to ask for "pure double mustard" and to insist on having it. She then knows what she is getting, and can rely on the article.

WHOLESOMENESS OF MUSTARD. In addition to its employment as a condiment at table, for use with such foods as beef, pork, and cheese, mustard has many other culinary uses. It is employed in making pickles and curry, and also plays a useful part in certain sauces.

Taken in sensibly moderate amounts, mustard is decidedly wholesome. It tends to increase the flow of the saliva and to whet the appetite. Moreover, it gives a flavour and attractive pungency to certain dishes—*e.g.,* cold meats, which, in themselves, are not very tasty and would, perhaps, not be enjoyed. It has to be always remembered that without enjoyment the digestive powers do not function properly.

On the other hand, as already indicated, the pungent principles liberated from mustard when treated with water, are physiologically very active. Indeed, the volatile oil of mustard is a distinctly dangerous substance to handle. As every housewife knows, a good dose of mustard in hot water is a powerful emetic, quite usefully employed when, for instance, a narcotic poison has been accidentally swallowed, whose immediate ejection from the stomach through the mouth is essential. It is obvious, therefore, that over-indulgence in mustard would be decidedly injurious; whereas, used reasonably, the amount of the active principles taken is so small that their action is rather beneficial than otherwise.

PEPPER

The name "pepper" has been applied to numerous aromatic and pungent spices, many of which, however, are of little or no interest to the British housewife. Jamaica pepper, more correctly called "pimento" or "allspice," is useful for flavouring soups, etc., and is a common ingredient of "mixed spice." For use at table as condiments in this country, however, only white pepper, black pepper, and varieties of Cayenne pepper are employed.

BLACK AND WHITE PEPPERS. White and black peppers are the products of one and the same plant. This is *Piper nigrum* L. (Natural Order, *Piperaceæ*), a climbing shrub, native to the Malabar coast of India and cultivated in many tropical countries, including India itself, where the pepper industry is an important one. Artificial or natural supports are provided for the pepper vines, which climb to a considerable height and produce an abundance of leaves, pointed at their ends, and masses of little fruits borne in spikes. As soon as the fruits begin to redden, they are plucked and dried in the sun, when they shrivel and blacken, the product constituting black pepper. Of course, before being used, the peppercorns, as they are called, have first to be ground.

When white pepper is required, the harvest is usually delayed a little for the fruit to ripen. The essential part of the process, however, consists in soaking the fruits in water for about a week, and then rubbing them to remove their outer, dark-coloured coatings. Sometimes special machinery is used for this purpose; but the older plan consists in treading the soaked fruits underneath the feet.

Pepper contains an alkaloid called "piperine," a pungent resin and a small amount of volatile oil, which gives it its characteristic aroma. Peppers coming from different districts vary a little in pungency and aroma, and are distinguished for trade purposes according to their places of origin. Black pepper has, in general, a fuller flavour than white pepper. Good quality ground pepper is made from a careful selection of different varieties chosen to give the best results. Adulteration of pepper is not extensively practised. Another species of pepper, known as "long pepper," of different aroma, was once used, along with entirely worthless materials, such as ground olive stones, etc. Practically complete protection from adulteration can be obtained by purchasing peppercorns and grinding these oneself in a small pepper-mill. This plan has the further advantage that freshly ground pepper has a better flavour than that which has been stored for some time.

WHOLESOMENESS AND USE OF PEPPER. Used as a condiment, pepper gives a decided zest to the flavour of starchy foods which otherwise tend to be rather insipid—*e.g.,* potatoes, cereals, etc. A light sprinkling of pepper is also found to be a palatable addition to a variety of other foods, including soups, fish dishes, egg dishes, melon, etc., etc., though in many cases the addition of pepper should be unnecessary after the dish has been served, if due attention has been paid to flavouring it during its preparation. Pepper is decidedly useful in the kitchen, and figures in numerous recipes as an essential or desirable ingredient.

The moderate use of pepper is to be commended, as pepper increases the flow of the saliva and gastric juices and thus tends to improve the appetite. Pepper possesses carminative properties, and helps to relieve flatulence.

At the same time, it has to be remembered that pepper contains a physiologically active alkaloid, piperine. Its action is to stimulate perspiration and thus to promote a fall in the temperature. For this reason, it is sometimes employed medicinally in the treatment of fevers (*e.g.,* malaria), and it is no doubt because of its final cooling effect that pepper is so much esteemed as a condiment in hot countries. Taken in small amounts, as a seasoning for food, pepper, therefore, is quite useful; but in large doses it would prove very irritating and injurious, so that over-indulgence in pepper, or indeed, in any condiment, is to be deprecated.

Red Peppers. Red, or Cayenne pepper, is quite distinct in origin from black and white peppers. Red and yellow peppers, of different sorts, including paprika or Hungarian pepper, and also sweet peppers, chillies and capsicums, are the fruits of various species of *Capsicum,* a genus of plants belonging to the Natural Order *Solanaceæ,* originally natives of Central and South America, but now spread practically all over the warmer parts of the world. There are probably two distinct species, as well as numerous varieties produced by cultivation.

Capsicum, as defined by *The British Pharmacopœia,* is the dried, ripe fruit of *Capsicum minimum* Roxb. This is employed medicinally; its taste is very pungent and acrid. Japanese chillies, which resemble this drug in appearance, but are somewhat larger, are the dried ripe fruits of *Capsicum frutescens* L. From these and allied varieties, the Cayenne peppers of commerce are mostly derived. They may be made simply by drying and powdering the fruits; or the powder may be mixed with flour, leavened with yeast, kneaded into small masses, baked hard, and reground. Not only does the product vary according to the variety of fruit employed, but also according to the method of treatment, *e.g.,* removal of certain parts, preliminary washing of the seed, etc.

In general, the larger fruits are less pungent than the smaller ones. Some varieties of *Capsicum annuum* L., produce fruits which are practically devoid of pungency. These are known as sweet peppers and are used as a vegetable.

Nepaul pepper is a highly esteemed variety of Cayenne pepper, and is yellow in colour. It has a very special flavour and is expensive. Paprika, or Hungarian pepper, is prepared from the fruits of *Capsicum annuum*, in five grades, which differ in quality, flavour and pungency. Spanish paprika or pimienta is very lacking in pungency, and is chiefly of use as a colouring agent.

WHOLESOMENESS AND USE OF CAYENNE PEPPER. The pungency of the red peppers is due to a specific substance, of which the hottest Cayenne contains only about one-fifth per cent., and most varieties much less. It will be appreciated, therefore, that this substance is most violently active physiologically. It is, indeed, poisonous. Cayenne pepper is such a pungent condiment, that it should not be necessary to point out that over-indulgence in it is injurious. Nevertheless, a little of it acts as a useful stimulant and carminative to the alimentary canal; and there are some dishes with which its extreme pungency excellently blends. It is quite a mistake, however, to attempt to use Cayenne pepper or paprika as a substitute for ordinary black or white pepper, as their flavours are quite distinct. Cayenne pepper, it may be mentioned, is sometimes used as an adulterant of mustard.

VINEGAR

VINEGAR is a liquid of sharp taste, which varies in colour from palest yellow or water-white to dark brown. It is much employed as a condiment at table and has still more uses in the kitchen.

The sharpness of vinegar is due to the presence in it of an acid called "acetic acid." Good vinegar should contain at least 4 per cent. of acetic acid; frequently the amount present is greater than this. Pure acetic acid is a very caustic liquid, which forms colourless crystals when cooled. In vinegar, the sharpness of the acid is mitigated by the large quantity of water present.

In addition to water and acetic acid, good vinegar also contains natural flavouring materials and (usually) colouring matter, sugar, etc.

The colour of vinegar is no guide to its quality whatever. Perfectly colourless artificial vinegar can easily be made and tinted to any desired shade with coal-tar dyes or with burnt sugar.

How Vinegar is Made. Undoubtedly, vinegar was first obtained through the natural souring of wine. It is now known that two things are necessary for this souring to take place; there must be free access of air, to supply the necessary oxygen, for acetic acid is a product of the oxidation of alcohol; and a specific bacillus must be present in order that the desired oxidation may take place.

These facts are utilised in the manufacture of genuine vinegar, which is always made by souring a weak form of alcoholic liquor.

In the old-fashioned slow process, the liquor is placed in casks half-filled with beech-shavings, which have been previously treated with vinegar and have hence become impregnated with the necessary bacillus. The bung holes are left open so that the air may get in, and the casks are preferably stored in a warm place. Many months must elapse before the alcoholic liquor is converted into vinegar.

In the modern, or rapid process, large vats are used, fitted with false bottoms. On these are placed beech-shavings, or pieces of pumice stone, coke, or other suitable material, which have been treated with vinegar, after cleansing, and have thus become impregnated with the bacillus. The alcoholic liquor is sprinkled on these from the top, and after running through slowly is pumped back again. Air is supplied by means of holes situated below the false bottoms. By this means the production of vinegar is effected much more rapidly, and takes only two or three weeks.

Chief Types of Vinegar. In France, vinegar is mostly made from inferior wines, the colour of the product depending on whether red or white wine is employed. Vinegar from white wine is considered superior to that from red wine. In England, vinegar is mostly made from malt. This is first of all fermented with yeast to produce a special kind of malt liquor, which, after storing, is converted into vinegar by the rapid process. Vinegar made from cider is used in the United States, and is also made to a small extent in Great Britain.

These vinegars are all good. They differ in their aromas according to the type of alcoholic liquor from which they have been made. The choice between wine vinegar, malt vinegar, and cider vinegar is, therefore, entirely a matter of taste. Malt vinegar is mostly preferred by English palates, and, failing any special taste or other reason, the British housewife will be well advised to ask for "pure malt vinegar" and to insist on having it.

This is specially important, as there are some other forms of vinegar made which, although cheaper than malt, wine, and cider vinegars, are much inferior to these and are liable to contain noxious impurities.

Artificial or wood vinegar is obtained from wood or similar sources and is most injurious to use. Spirit vinegar is made from diluted alcohol, but the latter may come from a tainted source; and, in any case, this sort of vinegar is destitute of aroma. Artificial flavouring matters, as well as artificial colouring matters, are often added to these inferior vinegars.

Uses of Vinegars. Vinegar is employed in making mint sauce and many other types of sauces, especially those to season fish dishes. It is also used for pickling, as a salad dressing, usually in combination with oil, mustard, pepper, salt, etc., and for adding a note of sharpness to the taste of certain soups. A drop or two added to milk used in cake-making is said to be distinctly advantageous, producing lighter cakes; and, in some cases (but by no means all) wine in recipes can be replaced by vinegar which has been well sweetened by the addition of sugar.

Although always placed on the dining table, there is, as a matter of fact, no great call for use of vinegar strictly in the sense of a condiment. Few dishes are improved by the addition of vinegar after they have been cooked, if skilfully prepared with a view to excellence of flavour. Vinegar, how-ever, may be advantageously added to spinach if prepared, as is often the case, without its aid; and is certainly desirable as an addition to fish which has been preserved in oil (sardines, etc.), and as a salad dressing.

Special, or spiced, vinegars are useful. These are made by flavouring good vinegar with suitable herbs or spices. One of the best herbs for this purpose and one most highly favoured is tarragon (*Artemisia Dracunculus* L.). Tarragon vinegar can be made by placing a quantity of freshly-picked, clean leaves of tarragon in a wide-mouthed bottle or stone jar, and covering them with good vinegar, preferably white wine vinegar. The bottle or jar should be quite full and its mouth should be tightly covered, so as to exclude air. The tarragon should be allowed to remain in the vinegar for at least six weeks, after which the vinegar should be poured off and strained, if necessary, through a piece of clean muslin.

WHOLESOMENESS OF VINEGAR. Vinegar made from wine, malt, or cider, is quite a wholesome material if used with sensible moderation. Acetic acid tends to promote, in a mild degree, perspiration and the passing of urine, though when taken with food in the form of vinegar, the amount of this acid is so small, that its action is very slight.

For some purposes, lemon juice may be used as a substitute for vinegar. The flavour of this, however, is not usually so much appreciated as is that of vinegar in those combinations in which we are accustomed to use the latter condiment. Moreover, although lemon juice contains the valuable vitamin C, its use, in the case of some people, is found to give rise to digestive troubles not observed when vinegar is employed.

SALT

CHEMISTS apply the word "salt" to an immense family of substances, some of which, such as "Glauber's Salt," Epsom salts, etc., are well known on account of their medicinal uses. Washing soda and sodium bicarbonate belong to this same family and are, strictly speaking, salts. But in the culinary art, we restrict the term to the material which is the commonest salt of all, since it occurs in vast quantities dissolved in sea-water and in the form of the mineral, rock salt, and as brine, deposited in numerous parts of the earth.

Naturally, it does not occur in these places in a state of purity, but in association with other mineral substances. The purity of the finished article depends not only upon the source, but also on the processes adopted for its production.

Pure salt, called by chemists "sodium chloride," is a compound of the two elements sodium and chlorine. It forms colourless, cubical crystals or a white crystalline powder, and is devoid of odour and hence of flavour, but has a very characteristic taste. It readily dissolves in cold water (about 1 in 3) and is only very slightly more soluble in boiling water.

MANUFACTURE OF TABLE SALT. At one time, the bulk of the salt in commerce was obtained by evaporating sea-water. But the product thus obtained is very impure, containing only about 78 per cent. of pure salt. The impurities give it a bitter taste and a purgative action if taken in sufficient amount.

To-day, salt for table use is obtained both from natural brine deposits and from deposits of rock salt, and the finished product is prepared in such a manner that the bulk of the impurities are removed.

In countries enjoying a warm climate, the heat of the sun may be utilised to evaporate the brine. The first crop of salt crystals is the best, and may contain about 96 per cent. of pure salt, the balance being largely moisture. Later crops of crystals are less pure.

In Great Britain and some other countries, where the heat of the sun is not adequate, the brine has to be evaporated by heat artificially applied, and, in some cases, certain impurities may be removed by appropriate chemical treatment. This is especially desirable when the brine (as in Ohio, U.S.A.) contains poisonous barium salts. Good brines, such as those of Droitwich (Worcestershire), contain about 25 per cent. of salt and under 1 per cent. of other substances.

Rock salt varies in purity. That occurring in Cheshire is estimated to contain a little over 98 per cent. of pure salt.

In some parts of the world, rock salt is found which is considered sufficiently pure for use without further treatment, and it is therefore merely ground and sieved. The more usual practice, however, as at Middlesbrough (Yorkshire), is to allow fresh water to run down bore-holes to the salt deposits. The resulting brine is then evaporated.

VARIETIES OF SALT. Small crystals are obtained by boiling the brine continuously; and many grades of salt are distinguished in the trade according to the method of preparation and consequent purity and the purpose for which the salt is intended. The coarsest grade is known as "bay salt" and usually contains about 10 per cent. of impurities.

Even the purest salt, except that specially prepared for use in delicate analytical operations, contains traces of impurities of a water-loving or "hygroscopic" character, in virtue of which the salt becomes damp if exposed to the air. To counteract this, traces of such substances as sodium phosphate or carbonate are often added to fine table salt.

USES OF SALT IN COOKING. If some brine is put in a vessel and some pure water carefully poured on top, it will be found, after a time, that some of the salt has passed or "diffused" into the top layer of water, making it quite salt. The force which drives the salt upwards from the brine into the pure water is called by chemists the "osmotic pressure," and is very important from the point of view of the cook.

It is possible, by means of special apparatus, to vary the above experiment by separating some brine from some pure water by a membrane or film which will let pure water pass through it, but not salt. In this case, water will gradually pass into the brine, making it weaker. We may say, therefore, that osmotic pressure is a force which tends to make a solution weaker, whenever this is possible.

This property of salt helps to explain why eating salt produces thirst; and to the same property the utility of salt in cooking is partly due. If we boil fish in plain water, most of the natural salts will be removed, and the fish will lack flavour. By adding a little salt to the water, however, the pressure set up tends to stop the diffusion of these salts. The same is true of pieces of freshly-cut meat. It is also a fact that potatoes cooked without salt are very flavourless, and the defect cannot be remedied by adding salt afterwards. As it is commonly said, adding salt during cooking helps "to bring out the flavour."

Moreover, certain combinations of flavour seem to require a *slight* taste of salt for their full enjoyment. The salt, like a discord in a harmony, gives point to the composition.

WHOLESOMENESS OF SALT. The elements of which salt is composed are both essential constituents of our bodies. These elements also occur, in general, in plants. It would seem, however, that herbivorous animals cannot obtain a sufficient supply of these from the plants they eat, since all or most of them require a little additional salt.

Salt, therefore, must be considered as a wholesome article of diet, and a most useful culinary material. At the same time, however, it may be questioned whether it is as necessary as a condiment for addition to foods at table as is commonly supposed. Salt is often used in this manner far in excess of our needs, which should, in general, be adequately met by the small amounts of salt naturally present in our foodstuffs and those added during cooking. Folk who cannot enjoy a meal without adding huge amounts of salt to each dish have blunted sensibilities for the appreciation of the finer and more delicate flavours; and it seems likely that over-indulgence in salt is liable to lead to such blunting. Persons afflicted with dropsy or kidney diseases are advised to avoid salt entirely.

There are some flavours which seem to blend especially well with the taste of salt. Celery is one of these, and salt flavoured with celery seed or a trace of the essential oil of celery seed is sometimes used as a condiment in place of ordinary salt.

Salt is also employed as a preservative, as for example, in salting fish. For this purpose, salt of a cruder character than table salt is used, and answers the purpose very well.

OIL

THE word "oil" is commonly applied to such a diversity of liquids, that it is practically impossible to give a general definition of its meaning which will cover all usages. From the point of view of the culinary art, however, two classes of oils are important. These are (a) the essential or volatile oils; and (b) the fixed oils of vegetable origin. The first group are liquids which are volatile or easily dissipated by heat, obtained mainly by distillation from sweet-smelling flowers, spices, and herbs. These oils are very aromatic and are used for making flavouring essences, perfumes, liqueurs, etc. The second group are non-volatile liquids of a fatty or greasy character. They may be described as liquid fats.

The latter oils are used in cooking, and a bottle of "salad oil," which is a suitable oil of this type, invariably accompanies the vinegar and other condiments on a well-laid table. It seems appropriate, therefore, to append a few details concerning the various oils used for the purpose.

OLIVE OIL. The oil most highly esteemed as a salad oil and for cooking is pure olive oil, preferably virgin oil, a term which is explained below.

The olive is the fruit of the Olive tree (*Olea europæa* L., Natural Order *Oleaceæ*), which was one of the first trees to be cultivated by mankind. It is an evergreen, native to the Mediterranean region, Syria, and Palestine, and is cultivated in these parts of the world and also in South Africa, Australia and California.

For the production of the finest quality olive oil, the fruits, when ripe, are picked by hand from selected trees grown in orchards. The oil is obtained by subjecting them to gentle pressure, care being taken not to crush the kernels. The oil thus obtained is called "virgin oil." The mass remaining behind is then ground up and subjected to further pressure, heat often being applied at the same time. An additional yield of oil is thereby obtained, but it is not so good as the virgin oil. A third yield of oil is sometimes got by treating the residue with a suitable solvent, such as carbon disulphide; but this oil is not fit for culinary use. Over-ripe fruit gives a bigger yield of oil, but the flavour is bad; whilst oil got from unripe fruits is apt to have a bitter taste.

Good olive oil should be pale yellow in colour and possess an agreeable and characteristic taste. A greenish colour usually denotes that the oil has been obtained from unripe fruits.

On cooling, olive oil congeals, its solidifying point varying from about $-6°$ to $+2°C$. The appearance of partly-congealed oil is not very agreeable; but the property is important as an indication of purity, though not an entirely reliable one. Housewives are advised to insist on "pure, virgin olive oil," and to refuse inferior qualities.

The chief constituent of olive oil is the liquid fat called "olein"; but the oil also contains other fatty substances, which are responsible for the ease with which it congeals.

Olive oil tends to go rancid, especially if exposed to the

air. It is advisable, therefore, to purchase it in small quantities at a time and to keep it in well-corked or stoppered bottles.

SWEET ALMOND OIL. Sweet almond oil may also be used for culinary purposes, and has the advantage of keeping better than olive oil. It is obtained by pressure from the kernels of both sweet and bitter almonds. The latter are more frequently used, as the mass remaining can be utilised for the production of the essential oil of bitter almonds. The last oil is poisonous, as it contains prussic acid, which, however, can be easily removed, as is always done when, for instance, the bitter almond oil is intended for making almond flavouring essence. The oil obtained by pressure, whether from sweet or bitter almonds, contains no prussic acid and is perfectly wholesome. Like olive oil, it consists chiefly of olein; but it has a different and more sweetly nutty flavour. The oil, however, is expensive, so that it is relatively little employed, even for pharmaceutical purposes. The oil expressed from apricot kernels forms a cheaper substitute, but does not keep so well.

POPPY SEED OIL. Poppy seed oil is another product used to some extent as a salad oil. Although this is obtained from the seeds of the Opium Poppy (*Papaver somniferum* L., Natural Order *Papaveraceæ*), neither the seeds nor the oil contain any opium or, indeed, anything of an injurious character. In some parts of Europe the seeds themselves are used as a filling for an agreeable form of pastry and might be so employed in Great Britain. Oil intended for use as a salad oil is obtained by pressure, without heat, and is afterwards filtered. It keeps remarkably well and has a characteristic and pleasant nutty taste. Inferior grades of poppy-seed oil should be avoided.

ARACHIS OR PEA-NUT OIL. The most important rival to

olive oil, however, is pea-nut or arachis oil, obtained by pressure, without heat, from pea-nuts. These are the seeds of *Arachis hypogæa* L., a member of the Natural Order *Leguminosæ* or Pea family. The plant is a native of Brazil; but it is cultivated in numerous tropical and sub-tropical countries, the most important British source being Gambia. The plant is not unlike a large clover in appearance. After the pods are formed, they turn downwards naturally and bury themselves in the ground, for which reason they are often known as "ground nuts."

The oil is a pale-yellow or greenish-yellow colour, and can be obtained quite colourless by bleaching. As in the case of olive oil, its chief constituent is olein. It has a slightly nutty taste, but, like all vegetable oils, tends to become rancid on keeping. It is cheaper than olive oil.

Arachis oil is quite wholesome, and its very mild flavour is well liked by many people. Epicures, however, prefer olive oil.

COTTON SEED AND OTHER OILS. Cotton seed oil is obtained by expression from the seeds of the plants, various species of *Gossypium* (Natural Order *Malvaceæ*), from which cotton is obtained, and which are cultivated in India, the U.S.A., Egypt, etc. The crude oil is dark in colour, but is refined for culinary use by appropriate chemical treatment, when it becomes yellowish. Refined oil is practically odourless, and has a bland, nutty taste.

In addition to olein, this oil contains a proportion of fatty substances which are normally solid. Hence it begins to congeal at a comparatively high temperature. It is a very common adulterant of and substitute for olive oil. Readers are strongly recommended not to use it as a salad oil, as it is too thick. It is, however, quite wholesome and suitable for frying.

Other vegetable oils used as salad oils, or as adulterants of olive oil, include sesame, gingelly or teel oil, maize oil, sunflower seed oil, etc.

WHOLESOMENESS OF OIL. There can be no doubt that the inclusion of a certain amount of olive or similar oil in the diet is very desirable. Although, as already mentioned, salad oil is always to be found on a well-laid table, too often it remains untouched; and most British housewives make far less use of oil in the kitchen than do their Continental sisters.

The oils mentioned are not only nutritious, but they also exercise a mildly laxative action. It is far better to drink a liqueur-glassful of olive or sweet almond oil than to take liquid (medicinal) paraffin, as a remedy for constipation; for the latter oil, being of mineral origin and quite alien in character to vegetable and animal fats and oils, is liable to interfere with the absorption of food. And it is pleasanter to take the olive or other suitable vegetable oil in the form of a dressed salad or other agreeable dish in which it has been skilfully incorporated.

On the other hand, it is an error to suppose that the vegetable oils can adequately take the place of the more solid animal fats in a well-balanced diet. Olive oil appears to be deficient in the fat-soluble vitamins. A balance between animal fats and vegetable oils is desirable.

COOKING UTENSILS

WHAT MATERIALS ARE BEST TO USE? A variety of materials are employed nowadays in the manufacture of cooking utensils; and, although, of course, all types of utensils cannot be made in every one of these, there is, nevertheless, a considerable variety from which the housewife may choose. Choosing aright is a matter of importance.

Copper utensils look very well if they are kept perfectly bright. They are, however, expensive and not much used in domestic kitchens. They need to be kept very clean. Otherwise, verdigris will form on them; and, although verdigris is not so poisonous as is sometimes supposed, it is a very undesirable material to get into food. The insides must be re-tinned whenever they show signs of wear.

Iron vessels are heavy and clumsy, and are not much used to-day. Wrought steel is preferable from the point of view of appearance, and vessels made of it are very durable, though the insides require to be re-tinned from time to time. Unlined iron saucepans, etc., are of very limited use, as iron is attacked by acid juices.

Enamelled ware is deservedly popular, as it is very clean in use, if properly employed. It is, however, of the utmost importance only to buy guaranteed articles of high quality, as some of the cheaper enamels are liable to contain highly poisonous substances. Care should be taken not to crack the enamel, which almost invariably happens if an empty saucepan or other vessel is placed over the fire or in the oven.

Aluminium is, to-day, one of the most popular materials.

Aluminium vessels are very light and easy to handle, food cooks rapidly in them, and, moreover, they have become much cheaper during the last few years. Nevertheless, aluminium is not an ideal material. Although this metal resists the action of acids rather well, it is easily acted on by alkalies. Therefore, nothing can be cooked in aluminium ware which requires the addition of carbonate of soda. Another drawback is that these vessels are not easy to keep clean, as they must not, of course, be scoured with soda.

In the case of acid foods, such as stewed fruit, tomatoes, etc., traces of aluminium are dissolved. But these are considered by most authorities to be too small to have an injurious effect on the health;* and their effect on the flavour is too slight for any but the most sensitive palates to detect.

Nevertheless, the housewife who desires to obtain the best results will make only limited use of aluminium utensils, and will, for all purposes for which such vessels can be obtained, use those of earthenware or fire-resisting glass.

Casserole cookery finds much favour amongst chefs in France, who have raised the culinary art to its highest pitch of perfection. Earthenware is a most clean material and can impart no flavour of its own to any food. It is important, however, to see that it is well glazed. Otherwise, it may abstract a flavour from food cooked in it and impart this to the next dish. For this reason, fire-resisting glass, which can be considered as a modern improvement on earthenware, is to be preferred, as it never exhibits this drawback. Moreover, cooking is effected more rapidly in glass than in earthenware. Fire-resisting glass utensils are not, however, quite so easy to clean as is sometimes claimed. But a little elbow-grease will always effect the desired result and enable

* *Vide* Editorials in *The Lancet*, Jan. 4th and Mar. 22nd, 1913; also E. E. Smith: *Aluminium Compounds in Food* (New York, 1928).

them to be kept in a spotless condition. Their transparency is an advantage, both from the point of view of cleanliness and because it facilitates examination of the food whilst being cooked.

CLEANING CULINARY UTENSILS. It is of the utmost importance that all utensils used for cooking and serving food should be kept scrupulously clean. If particles of food are allowed to adhere to pots and pans, not only will the flavour of everything cooked in them be marred, but health may be endangered.

Exposed to the air, most foods become infected with bacteria, which bring about their decomposition. Not all these bacteria are harmful to health. For example, the bacteria producing lactic acid fermentation in milk, whereby youghourt (which is a Bulgarian fermented milk) is made, is quite beneficial. But many of these bacteria, especially those which attack meat and fish, are very injurious. Moreover, there are some bacteria which are able to function in the absence of air, such as the bacillus of botulism—a form of poisoning caused by imperfectly cooked ham and sausages—and these, perhaps, are the most dangerous of all. This is the reason why improperly canned food is so dangerous. Properly canned food, which has been completely sterilised at the moment of canning, however, is harmless, though inferior in flavour to fresh food.

It was at one time believed that food poisoning was due to certain substances of a basic character, allied to the alkaloids, produced by the decomposition of proteins. These were called "ptomaines." However, it is now realised that the causation of food poisoning is of a more complex character, and the expression "ptomaine poisoning" has largely dropped out of scientific usage. Poisoning may be due to poisons formed by bacterial decomposition of food, or it may be due—and cases of this are the more serious—to living bacteria themselves gaining entrance to our bodies. In any event, the need for cleanliness is paramount.

The materials used for cleaning culinary utensils may be classified as under:—

ABRASIVES. These are rough materials, such as silver sand, brick dust, pumice stone, etc., which enable stains, etc., to be removed by mechanical friction. Wire brushes and steel shavings also constitute useful cleansing materials of this type.

SOAP. Soap exercises a special action on oils and fats, loosening them and enabling them to mix with water to form emulsions or milky liquids. Soap is, therefore, extremely useful for cleaning greasy dishes. It is more effective if used with hot water which has been softened by the addition of soda or other water softener, as the lime in hard water interferes with its action.

ALKALIES. The chief of these is washing soda. This has a solvent action on grease and softens hard water. Its disadvantage is that it has a very harsh action on the skin. This can be remedied, to some extent, by plunging the hands into water acidified with vinegar or lemon juice, immediately after washing up. There are, however, now on the market, several proprietary cleansing powders which have useful properties like soda, but are free from its harshness. Some of these contain also abrasives. Ashes act similarly to soda. Neither should be used for cleaning aluminium. It is best in this case to use a little silver sand, but not to scour too hard, as the brown film which forms constitutes a protective coating.

ACIDS. Weak acids, such as vinegar and especially lemon juice, are decidedly useful for removing stains from enamelled ware, owing to their solvent action. They are more effective if used in conjunction with salt, a portion of lemon sprinkled with salt being a convenient form in which to employ the combination.

DRYING CULINARY UTENSILS. After they have been cleansed, all culinary utensils should be thoroughly dried. If left wet, metal utensils will oxidise. Copper will become coated with verdigris, iron with rust, and aluminium with a coating of white aluminium oxide. This last is just as objectionable as iron rust; but, as it is not so unsightly, the housewife is too apt to ignore it, with detrimental results to the quality and flavour of the meals she prepares.

INDEX

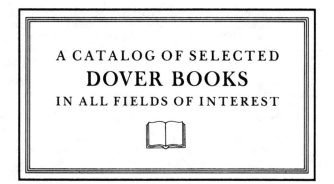

A CATALOG OF SELECTED
DOVER BOOKS
IN ALL FIELDS OF INTEREST

A CATALOG OF SELECTED DOVER BOOKS IN ALL FIELDS OF INTEREST

DRAWINGS OF REMBRANDT, edited by Seymour Slive. Updated Lippmann, Hofstede de Groot edition, with definitive scholarly apparatus. All portraits, biblical sketches, landscapes, nudes. Oriental figures, classical studies, together with selection of work by followers. 550 illustrations. Total of 630pp. 9⅛ × 12¼.
21485-0, 21486-9 Pa., Two-vol. set $25.00

GHOST AND HORROR STORIES OF AMBROSE BIERCE, Ambrose Bierce. 24 tales vividly imagined, strangely prophetic, and decades ahead of their time in technical skill: "The Damned Thing," "An Inhabitant of Carcosa," "The Eyes of the Panther," "Moxon's Master," and 20 more. 199pp. 5⅜ × 8½. 20767-6 Pa. $3.95

ETHICAL WRITINGS OF MAIMONIDES, Maimonides. Most significant ethical works of great medieval sage, newly translated for utmost precision, readability. Laws Concerning Character Traits, Eight Chapters, more. 192pp. 5⅜ × 8½.
24522-5 Pa. $4.50

THE EXPLORATION OF THE COLORADO RIVER AND ITS CANYONS, J. W. Powell. Full text of Powell's 1,000-mile expedition down the fabled Colorado in 1869. Superb account of terrain, geology, vegetation, Indians, famine, mutiny, treacherous rapids, mighty canyons, during exploration of last unknown part of continental U.S. 400pp. 5⅜ × 8½. 20094-9 Pa. $6.95

HISTORY OF PHILOSOPHY, Julián Marías. Clearest one-volume history on the market. Every major philosopher and dozens of others, to Existentialism and later. 505pp. 5⅜ × 8½. 21739-6 Pa. $8.50

ALL ABOUT LIGHTNING, Martin A. Uman. Highly readable non-technical survey of nature and causes of lightning, thunderstorms, ball lightning, St. Elmo's Fire, much more. Illustrated. 192pp. 5⅜ × 8½. 25237-X Pa. $5.95

SAILING ALONE AROUND THE WORLD, Captain Joshua Slocum. First man to sail around the world, alone, in small boat. One of great feats of seamanship told in delightful manner. 67 illustrations. 294pp. 5⅜ × 8½. 20326-3 Pa. $4.95

LETTERS AND NOTES ON THE MANNERS, CUSTOMS AND CONDITIONS OF THE NORTH AMERICAN INDIANS, George Catlin. Classic account of life among Plains Indians: ceremonies, hunt, warfare, etc. 312 plates. 572pp. of text. 6⅛ × 9¼. 22118-0, 22119-9 Pa. Two-vol. set $15.90

ALASKA: The Harriman Expedition, 1899, John Burroughs, John Muir, et al. Informative, engrossing accounts of two-month, 9,000-mile expedition. Native peoples, wildlife, forests, geography, salmon industry, glaciers, more. Profusely illustrated. 240 black-and-white line drawings. 124 black-and-white photographs. 3 maps. Index. 576pp. 5⅜ × 8½. 25109-8 Pa. $11.95

THE BOOK OF BEASTS: Being a Translation from a Latin Bestiary of the Twelfth Century, T. H. White. Wonderful catalog real and fanciful beasts: manticore, griffin, phoenix, amphivius, jaculus, many more. White's witty erudite commentary on scientific, historical aspects. Fascinating glimpse of medieval mind. Illustrated. 296pp. 5⅜ × 8¼. (Available in U.S. only) 24609-4 Pa. $5.95

FRANK LLOYD WRIGHT: ARCHITECTURE AND NATURE With 160 Illustrations, Donald Hoffmann. Profusely illustrated study of influence of nature—especially prairie—on Wright's designs for Fallingwater, Robie House, Guggenheim Museum, other masterpieces. 96pp. 9¼ × 10¾. 25098-9 Pa. $7.95

FRANK LLOYD WRIGHT'S FALLINGWATER, Donald Hoffmann. Wright's famous waterfall house: planning and construction of organic idea. History of site, owners, Wright's personal involvement. Photographs of various stages of building. Preface by Edgar Kaufmann, Jr. 100 illustrations. 112pp. 9¼ × 10. 23671-4 Pa. $7.95

YEARS WITH FRANK LLOYD WRIGHT: Apprentice to Genius, Edgar Tafel. Insightful memoir by a former apprentice presents a revealing portrait of Wright the man, the inspired teacher, the greatest American architect. 372 black-and-white illustrations. Preface. Index. vi + 228pp. 8¼ × 11. 24801-1 Pa. $9.95

THE STORY OF KING ARTHUR AND HIS KNIGHTS, Howard Pyle. Enchanting version of King Arthur fable has delighted generations with imaginative narratives of exciting adventures and unforgettable illustrations by the author. 41 illustrations. xviii + 313pp. 6⅛ × 9¼. 21445-1 Pa. $6.50

THE GODS OF THE EGYPTIANS, E. A. Wallis Budge. Thorough coverage of numerous gods of ancient Egypt by foremost Egyptologist. Information on evolution of cults, rites and gods; the cult of Osiris; the Book of the Dead and its rites; the sacred animals and birds; Heaven and Hell; and more. 956pp. 6⅛ × 9¼. 22055-9, 22056-7 Pa., Two-vol. set $20.00

A THEOLOGICO-POLITICAL TREATISE, Benedict Spinoza. Also contains unfinished *Political Treatise*. Great classic on religious liberty, theory of government on common consent. R. Elwes translation. Total of 421pp. 5⅜ × 8½. 20249-6 Pa. $6.95

INCIDENTS OF TRAVEL IN CENTRAL AMERICA, CHIAPAS, AND YUCATAN, John L. Stephens. Almost single-handed discovery of Maya culture; exploration of ruined cities, monuments, temples; customs of Indians. 115 drawings. 892pp. 5⅜ × 8½. 22404-X, 22405-8 Pa., Two-vol. set $15.90

LOS CAPRICHOS, Francisco Goya. 80 plates of wild, grotesque monsters and caricatures. Prado manuscript included. 183pp. 6⅝ × 9⅝. 22384-1 Pa. $4.95

AUTOBIOGRAPHY: The Story of My Experiments with Truth, Mohandas K. Gandhi. Not hagiography, but Gandhi in his own words. Boyhood, legal studies, purification, the growth of the Satyagraha (nonviolent protest) movement. Critical, inspiring work of the man who freed India. 480pp. 5⅜ × 8½. (Available in U.S. only) 24593-4 Pa. $6.95

ILLUSTRATED DICTIONARY OF HISTORIC ARCHITECTURE, edited by Cyril M. Harris. Extraordinary compendium of clear, concise definitions for over 5,000 important architectural terms complemented by over 2,000 line drawings. Covers full spectrum of architecture from ancient ruins to 20th-century Modernism. Preface. 592pp. 7½ × 9⅜. 24444-X Pa. $14.95

THE NIGHT BEFORE CHRISTMAS, Clement Moore. Full text, and woodcuts from original 1848 book. Also critical, historical material. 19 illustrations. 40pp. 4⅝ × 6. 22797-9 Pa. $2.25

THE LESSON OF JAPANESE ARCHITECTURE: 165 Photographs, Jiro Harada. Memorable gallery of 165 photographs taken in the 1930's of exquisite Japanese homes of the well-to-do and historic buildings. 13 line diagrams. 192pp. 8⅜ × 11¼. 24778-3 Pa. $8.95

THE AUTOBIOGRAPHY OF CHARLES DARWIN AND SELECTED LET-TERS, edited by Francis Darwin. The fascinating life of eccentric genius composed of an intimate memoir by Darwin (intended for his children); commentary by his son, Francis; hundreds of fragments from notebooks, journals, papers; and letters to and from Lyell, Hooker, Huxley, Wallace and Henslow. xi + 365pp. 5⅜ × 8.
20479-0 Pa. $6.95

WONDERS OF THE SKY: Observing Rainbows, Comets, Eclipses, the Stars and Other Phenomena, Fred Schaaf. Charming, easy-to-read poetic guide to all manner of celestial events visible to the naked eye. Mock suns, glories, Belt of Venus, more. Illustrated. 299pp. 5¼ × 8¼. 24402-4 Pa. $7.95

BURNHAM'S CELESTIAL HANDBOOK, Robert Burnham, Jr. Thorough guide to the stars beyond our solar system. Exhaustive treatment. Alphabetical by constellation: Andromeda to Cetus in Vol. 1; Chamaeleon to Orion in Vol. 2; and Pavo to Vulpecula in Vol. 3. Hundreds of illustrations. Index in Vol. 3. 2,000pp. 6⅛ × 9¼. 23567-X, 23568-8, 23673-0 Pa., Three-vol. set $38.85

STAR NAMES: Their Lore and Meaning, Richard Hinckley Allen. Fascinating history of names various cultures have given to constellations and literary and folkloristic uses that have been made of stars. Indexes to subjects. Arabic and Greek names. Biblical references. Bibliography. 563pp. 5⅜ × 8½. 21079-0 Pa. $7.95

THIRTY YEARS THAT SHOOK PHYSICS: The Story of Quantum Theory, George Gamow. Lucid, accessible introduction to influential theory of energy and matter. Careful explanations of Dirac's anti-particles, Bohr's model of the atom, much more. 12 plates. Numerous drawings. 240pp. 5⅜ × 8½. 24895-X Pa. $4.95

CHINESE DOMESTIC FURNITURE IN PHOTOGRAPHS AND MEASURED DRAWINGS, Gustav Ecke. A rare volume, now affordably priced for antique collectors, furniture buffs and art historians. Detailed review of styles ranging from early Shang to late Ming. Unabridged republication. 161 black-and-white drawings, photos. Total of 224pp. 8⅜ × 11¼. (Available in U.S. only) 25171-3 Pa. $12.95

VINCENT VAN GOGH: A Biography, Julius Meier-Graefe. Dynamic, penetrating study of artist's life, relationship with brother, Theo, painting techniques, travels, more. Readable, engrossing. 160pp. 5⅜ × 8½. (Available in U.S. only)
25253-1 Pa. $3.95

HOW TO WRITE, Gertrude Stein. Gertrude Stein claimed anyone could understand her unconventional writing—here are clues to help. Fascinating improvisations, language experiments, explanations illuminate Stein's craft and the art of writing. Total of 414pp. 4⅜ × 6⅜. 23144-5 Pa. $5.95

ADVENTURES AT SEA IN THE GREAT AGE OF SAIL: Five Firsthand Narratives, edited by Elliot Snow. Rare true accounts of exploration, whaling, shipwreck, fierce natives, trade, shipboard life, more. 33 illustrations. Introduction. 353pp. 5⅜ × 8½. 25177-2 Pa. $7.95

THE HERBAL OR GENERAL HISTORY OF PLANTS, John Gerard. Classic descriptions of about 2,850 plants—with over 2,700 illustrations—includes Latin and English names, physical descriptions, varieties, time and place of growth, more. 2,706 illustrations. xlv + 1,678pp. 8½ × 12¼. 23147-X Cloth. $75.00

DOROTHY AND THE WIZARD IN OZ, L. Frank Baum. Dorothy and the Wizard visit the center of the Earth, where people are vegetables, glass houses grow and Oz characters reappear. Classic sequel to *Wizard of Oz*. 256pp. 5⅜ × 8. 24714-7 Pa. $4.95

SONGS OF EXPERIENCE: Facsimile Reproduction with 26 Plates in Full Color, William Blake. This facsimile of Blake's original "Illuminated Book" reproduces 26 full-color plates from a rare 1826 edition. Includes "The Tyger," "London," "Holy Thursday," and other immortal poems. 26 color plates. Printed text of poems. 48pp. 5¼ × 7. 24636-1 Pa. $3.50

SONGS OF INNOCENCE, William Blake. The first and most popular of Blake's famous "Illuminated Books," in a facsimile edition reproducing all 31 brightly colored plates. Additional printed text of each poem. 64pp. 5¼ × 7. 22764-2 Pa. $3.50

PRECIOUS STONES, Max Bauer. Classic, thorough study of diamonds, rubies, emeralds, garnets, etc.: physical character, occurrence, properties, use, similar topics. 20 plates, 8 in color. 94 figures. 659pp. 6⅛ × 9¼. 21910-0, 21911-9 Pa., Two-vol. set $15.90

ENCYCLOPEDIA OF VICTORIAN NEEDLEWORK, S. F. A. Caulfeild and Blanche Saward. Full, precise descriptions of stitches, techniques for dozens of needlecrafts—most exhaustive reference of its kind. Over 800 figures. Total of 679pp. 8⅛ × 11. Two volumes. Vol. 1 22800-2 Pa. $11.95
Vol. 2 22801-0 Pa. $11.95

THE MARVELOUS LAND OF OZ, L. Frank Baum. Second Oz book, the Scarecrow and Tin Woodman are back with hero named Tip, Oz magic. 136 illustrations. 287pp. 5⅜ × 8½. 20692-0 Pa. $5.95

WILD FOWL DECOYS, Joel Barber. Basic book on the subject, by foremost authority and collector. Reveals history of decoy making and rigging, place in American culture, different kinds of decoys, how to make them, and how to use them. 140 plates. 156pp. 7⅞ × 10¾. 20011-6 Pa. $8.95

HISTORY OF LACE, Mrs. Bury Palliser. Definitive, profusely illustrated chronicle of lace from earliest times to late 19th century. Laces of Italy, Greece, England, France, Belgium, etc. Landmark of needlework scholarship. 266 illustrations. 672pp. 6⅛ × 9¼. 24742-2 Pa. $14.95

ILLUSTRATED GUIDE TO SHAKER FURNITURE, Robert Meader. All furniture and appurtenances, with much on unknown local styles. 235 photos. 146pp. 9 × 12. 22819-3 Pa. $7.95

WHALE SHIPS AND WHALING: A Pictorial Survey, George Francis Dow. Over 200 vintage engravings, drawings, photographs of barks, brigs, cutters, other vessels. Also harpoons, lances, whaling guns, many other artifacts. Comprehensive text by foremost authority. 207 black-and-white illustrations. 288pp. 6 × 9. 24808-9 Pa. $8.95

THE BERTRAMS, Anthony Trollope. Powerful portrayal of blind self-will and thwarted ambition includes one of Trollope's most heartrending love stories. 497pp. 5⅜ × 8½. 25119-5 Pa. $8.95

ADVENTURES WITH A HAND LENS, Richard Headstrom. Clearly written guide to observing and studying flowers and grasses, fish scales, moth and insect wings, egg cases, buds, feathers, seeds, leaf scars, moss, molds, ferns, common crystals, etc.—all with an ordinary, inexpensive magnifying glass. 209 exact line drawings aid in your discoveries. 220pp. 5⅜ × 8½. 23330-8 Pa. $3.95

RODIN ON ART AND ARTISTS, Auguste Rodin. Great sculptor's candid, wide-ranging comments on meaning of art; great artists; relation of sculpture to poetry, painting, music; philosophy of life, more. 76 superb black-and-white illustrations of Rodin's sculpture, drawings and prints. 119pp. 8⅜ × 11¼. 24487-3 Pa. $6.95

FIFTY CLASSIC FRENCH FILMS, 1912–1982: A Pictorial Record, Anthony Slide. Memorable stills from Grand Illusion, Beauty and the Beast, Hiroshima, Mon Amour, many more. Credits, plot synopses, reviews, etc. 160pp. 8¼ × 11. 25256-6 Pa. $11.95

THE PRINCIPLES OF PSYCHOLOGY, William James. Famous long course complete, unabridged. Stream of thought, time perception, memory, experimental methods; great work decades ahead of its time. 94 figures. 1,391pp. 5⅜ × 8½. 20381-6, 20382-4 Pa., Two-vol. set $19.90

BODIES IN A BOOKSHOP, R. T. Campbell. Challenging mystery of blackmail and murder with ingenious plot and superbly drawn characters. In the best tradition of British suspense fiction. 192pp. 5⅜ × 8½. 24720-1 Pa. $3.95

CALLAS: PORTRAIT OF A PRIMA DONNA, George Jellinek. Renowned commentator on the musical scene chronicles incredible career and life of the most controversial, fascinating, influential operatic personality of our time. 64 black-and-white photographs. 416pp. 5⅜ × 8¼. 25047-4 Pa. $7.95

GEOMETRY, RELATIVITY AND THE FOURTH DIMENSION, Rudolph Rucker. Exposition of fourth dimension, concepts of relativity as Flatland characters continue adventures. Popular, easily followed yet accurate, profound. 141 illustrations. 133pp. 5⅜ × 8½. 23400-2 Pa. $3.95

HOUSEHOLD STORIES BY THE BROTHERS GRIMM, with pictures by Walter Crane. 53 classic stories—Rumpelstiltskin, Rapunzel, Hansel and Gretel, the Fisherman and his Wife, Snow White, Tom Thumb, Sleeping Beauty, Cinderella, and so much more—lavishly illustrated with original 19th century drawings. 114 illustrations. x + 269pp. 5⅜ × 8½. 21080-4 Pa. $4.50

SUNDIALS, Albert Waugh. Far and away the best, most thorough coverage of ideas, mathematics concerned, types, construction, adjusting anywhere. Over 100 illustrations. 230pp. 5⅜ × 8½. 22947-5 Pa. $4.50

PICTURE HISTORY OF THE NORMANDIE: With 190 Illustrations, Frank O. Braynard. Full story of legendary French ocean liner: Art Deco interiors, design innovations, furnishings, celebrities, maiden voyage, tragic fire, much more. Extensive text. 144pp. 8⅜ × 11¾. 25257-4 Pa. $9.95

THE FIRST AMERICAN COOKBOOK: A Facsimile of "American Cookery," 1796, Amelia Simmons. Facsimile of the first American-written cookbook published in the United States contains authentic recipes for colonial favorites—pumpkin pudding, winter squash pudding, spruce beer, Indian slapjacks, and more. Introductory Essay and Glossary of colonial cooking terms. 80pp. 5⅜ × 8½. 24710-4 Pa. $3.50

101 PUZZLES IN THOUGHT AND LOGIC, C. R. Wylie, Jr. Solve murders and robberies, find out which fishermen are liars, how a blind man could possibly identify a color—purely by your own reasoning! 107pp. 5⅜ × 8½. 20367-0 Pa. $2.50

THE BOOK OF WORLD-FAMOUS MUSIC—CLASSICAL, POPULAR AND FOLK, James J. Fuld. Revised and enlarged republication of landmark work in musico-bibliography. Full information about nearly 1,000 songs and compositions including first lines of music and lyrics. New supplement. Index. 800pp. 5⅜ × 8¼. 24857-7 Pa. $14.95

ANTHROPOLOGY AND MODERN LIFE, Franz Boas. Great anthropologist's classic treatise on race and culture. Introduction by Ruth Bunzel. Only inexpensive paperback edition. 255pp. 5⅜ × 8½. 25245-0 Pa. $5.95

THE TALE OF PETER RABBIT, Beatrix Potter. The inimitable Peter's terrifying adventure in Mr. McGregor's garden, with all 27 wonderful, full-color Potter illustrations. 55pp. 4¼ × 5½. (Available in U.S. only) 22827-4 Pa. $1.75

THREE PROPHETIC SCIENCE FICTION NOVELS, H. G. Wells. *When the Sleeper Wakes, A Story of the Days to Come* and *The Time Machine* (full version). 335pp. 5⅜ × 8½. (Available in U.S. only) 20605-X Pa. $5.95

APICIUS COOKERY AND DINING IN IMPERIAL ROME, edited and translated by Joseph Dommers Vehling. Oldest known cookbook in existence offers readers a clear picture of what foods Romans ate, how they prepared them, etc. 49 illustrations. 301pp. 6⅛ × 9¼. 23563-7 Pa. $6.50

SHAKESPEARE LEXICON AND QUOTATION DICTIONARY, Alexander Schmidt. Full definitions, locations, shades of meaning of every word in plays and poems. More than 50,000 exact quotations. 1,485pp. 6½ × 9¼. 22726-X, 22727-8 Pa., Two-vol. set $27.90

THE WORLD'S GREAT SPEECHES, edited by Lewis Copeland and Lawrence W. Lamm. Vast collection of 278 speeches from Greeks to 1970. Powerful and effective models; unique look at history. 842pp. 5⅜ × 8½. 20468-5 Pa. $11.95

THE BLUE FAIRY BOOK, Andrew Lang. The first, most famous collection, with many familiar tales: Little Red Riding Hood, Aladdin and the Wonderful Lamp, Puss in Boots, Sleeping Beauty, Hansel and Gretel, Rumpelstiltskin; 37 in all. 138 illustrations. 390pp. 5⅜ × 8½. 21437-0 Pa. $5.95

THE STORY OF THE CHAMPIONS OF THE ROUND TABLE, Howard Pyle. Sir Launcelot, Sir Tristram and Sir Percival in spirited adventures of love and triumph retold in Pyle's inimitable style. 50 drawings, 31 full-page. xviii + 329pp. 6½ × 9¼. 21883-X Pa. $6.95

AUDUBON AND HIS JOURNALS, Maria Audubon. Unmatched two-volume portrait of the great artist, naturalist and author contains his journals, an excellent biography by his granddaughter, expert annotations by the noted ornithologist, Dr. Elliott Coues, and 37 superb illustrations. Total of 1,200pp. 5⅜ × 8.
Vol. I 25143-8 Pa. $8.95
Vol. II 25144-6 Pa. $8.95

GREAT DINOSAUR HUNTERS AND THEIR DISCOVERIES, Edwin H. Colbert. Fascinating, lavishly illustrated chronicle of dinosaur research, 1820's to 1960. Achievements of Cope, Marsh, Brown, Buckland, Mantell, Huxley, many others. 384pp. 5¼ × 8¼. 24701-5 Pa. $6.95

THE TASTEMAKERS, Russell Lynes. Informal, illustrated social history of American taste 1850's–1950's. First popularized categories Highbrow, Lowbrow, Middlebrow. 129 illustrations. New (1979) afterword. 384pp. 6 × 9.
23993-4 Pa. $6.95

DOUBLE CROSS PURPOSES, Ronald A. Knox. A treasure hunt in the Scottish Highlands, an old map, unidentified corpse, surprise discoveries keep reader guessing in this cleverly intricate tale of financial skullduggery. 2 black-and-white maps. 320pp. 5⅜ × 8½. (Available in U.S. only) 25032-6 Pa. $5.95

AUTHENTIC VICTORIAN DECORATION AND ORNAMENTATION IN FULL COLOR: 46 Plates from "Studies in Design," Christopher Dresser. Superb full-color lithographs reproduced from rare original portfolio of a major Victorian designer. 48pp. 9¼ × 12¼. 25083-0 Pa. $7.95

PRIMITIVE ART, Franz Boas. Remains the best text ever prepared on subject, thoroughly discussing Indian, African, Asian, Australian, and, especially, North-ern American primitive art. Over 950 illustrations show ceramics, masks, totem poles, weapons, textiles, paintings, much more. 376pp. 5⅜ × 8. 20025-6 Pa. $6.95

SIDELIGHTS ON RELATIVITY, Albert Einstein. Unabridged republication of two lectures delivered by the great physicist in 1920–21. *Ether and Relativity* and *Geometry and Experience*. Elegant ideas in non-mathematical form, accessible to intelligent layman. vi + 56pp. 5⅜ × 8½. 24511-X Pa. $2.95

THE WIT AND HUMOR OF OSCAR WILDE, edited by Alvin Redman. More than 1,000 ripostes, paradoxes, wisecracks: Work is the curse of the drinking classes, I can resist everything except temptation, etc. 258pp. 5⅜ × 8½. 20602-5 Pa. $4.50

ADVENTURES WITH A MICROSCOPE, Richard Headstrom. 59 adventures with clothing fibers, protozoa, ferns and lichens, roots and leaves, much more. 142 illustrations. 232pp. 5⅜ × 8½. 23471-1 Pa. $3.95

PLANTS OF THE BIBLE, Harold N. Moldenke and Alma L. Moldenke. Standard reference to all 230 plants mentioned in Scriptures. Latin name, biblical reference, uses, modern identity, much more. Unsurpassed encyclopedic resource for scholars, botanists, nature lovers, students of Bible. Bibliography. Indexes. 123 black-and-white illustrations. 384pp. 6 × 9. 25069-5 Pa. $8.95

FAMOUS AMERICAN WOMEN: A Biographical Dictionary from Colonial Times to the Present, Robert McHenry, ed. From Pocahontas to Rosa Parks, 1,035 distinguished American women documented in separate biographical entries. Accurate, up-to-date data, numerous categories, spans 400 years. Indices. 493pp. 6½ × 9¼. 24523-3 Pa. $9.95

THE FABULOUS INTERIORS OF THE GREAT OCEAN LINERS IN HISTORIC PHOTOGRAPHS, William H. Miller, Jr. Some 200 superb photographs capture exquisite interiors of world's great "floating palaces"—1890's to 1980's: *Titanic, Ile de France, Queen Elizabeth, United States, Europa,* more. Approx. 200 black-and-white photographs. Captions. Text. Introduction. 160pp. 8⅜ × 11¼. 24756-2 Pa. $9.95

THE GREAT LUXURY LINERS, 1927-1954: A Photographic Record, William H. Miller, Jr. Nostalgic tribute to heyday of ocean liners. 186 photos of Ile de France, Normandie, Leviathan, Queen Elizabeth, United States, many others. Interior and exterior views. Introduction. Captions. 160pp. 9 × 12. 24056-8 Pa. $9.95

A NATURAL HISTORY OF THE DUCKS, John Charles Phillips. Great landmark of ornithology offers complete detailed coverage of nearly 200 species and subspecies of ducks: gadwall, sheldrake, merganser, pintail, many more. 74 full-color plates, 102 black-and-white. Bibliography. Total of 1,920pp. 8⅜ × 11¼. 25141-1, 25142-X Cloth. Two-vol. set $100.00

THE SEAWEED HANDBOOK: An Illustrated Guide to Seaweeds from North Carolina to Canada, Thomas F. Lee. Concise reference covers 78 species. Scientific and common names, habitat, distribution, more. Finding keys for easy identification. 224pp. 5⅜ × 8½. 25215-9 Pa. $5.95

THE TEN BOOKS OF ARCHITECTURE: The 1755 Leoni Edition, Leon Battista Alberti. Rare classic helped introduce the glories of ancient architecture to the Renaissance. 68 black-and-white plates. 336pp. 8⅜ × 11¼. 25239-6 Pa. $14.95

MISS MACKENZIE, Anthony Trollope. Minor masterpieces by Victorian master unmasks many truths about life in 19th-century England. First inexpensive edition in years. 392pp. 5⅜ × 8½. 25201-9 Pa. $7.95

THE RIME OF THE ANCIENT MARINER, Gustave Doré, Samuel Taylor Coleridge. Dramatic engravings considered by many to be his greatest work. The terrifying space of the open sea, the storms and whirlpools of an unknown ocean, the ice of Antarctica, more—all rendered in a powerful, chilling manner. Full text. 38 plates. 77pp. 9¼ × 12. 22305-1 Pa. $4.95

THE EXPEDITIONS OF ZEBULON MONTGOMERY PIKE, Zebulon Montgomery Pike. Fascinating first-hand accounts (1805-6) of exploration of Mississippi River, Indian wars, capture by Spanish dragoons, much more. 1,088pp. 5⅜ × 8½. 25254-X, 25255-8 Pa. Two-vol. set $23.90

CATALOG OF DOVER BOOKS

A CONCISE HISTORY OF PHOTOGRAPHY: Third Revised Edition, Helmut Gernsheim. Best one-volume history—camera obscura, photochemistry, daguerreotypes, evolution of cameras, film, more. Also artistic aspects—landscape, portraits, fine art, etc. 281 black-and-white photographs. 26 in color. 176pp. 8⅜ × 11¼. 25128-4 Pa. $12.95

THE DORÉ BIBLE ILLUSTRATIONS, Gustave Doré. 241 detailed plates from the Bible: the Creation scenes, Adam and Eve, Flood, Babylon, battle sequences, life of Jesus, etc. Each plate is accompanied by the verses from the King James version of the Bible. 241pp. 9 × 12. 23004-X Pa. $8.95

HUGGER-MUGGER IN THE LOUVRE, Elliot Paul. Second Homer Evans mystery-comedy. Theft at the Louvre involves sleuth in hilarious, madcap caper. "A knockout."—Books. 336pp. 5⅜ × 8½. 25185-3 Pa. $5.95

FLATLAND, E. A. Abbott. Intriguing and enormously popular science-fiction classic explores the complexities of trying to survive as a two-dimensional being in a three-dimensional world. Amusingly illustrated by the author. 16 illustrations. 103pp. 5⅜ × 8½. 20001-9 Pa. $2.25

THE HISTORY OF THE LEWIS AND CLARK EXPEDITION, Meriwether Lewis and William Clark, edited by Elliott Coues. Classic edition of Lewis and Clark's day-by-day journals that later became the basis for U.S. claims to Oregon and the West. Accurate and invaluable geographical, botanical, biological, meteorological and anthropological material. Total of 1,508pp. 5⅜ × 8½.
21268-8, 21269-6, 21270-X Pa. Three-vol. set $25.50

LANGUAGE, TRUTH AND LOGIC, Alfred J. Ayer. Famous, clear introduction to Vienna, Cambridge schools of Logical Positivism. Role of philosophy, elimination of metaphysics, nature of analysis, etc. 160pp. 5⅜ × 8½. (Available in U.S. and Canada only) 20010-8 Pa. $2.95

MATHEMATICS FOR THE NONMATHEMATICIAN, Morris Kline. Detailed, college-level treatment of mathematics in cultural and historical context, with numerous exercises. For liberal arts students. Preface. Recommended Reading Lists. Tables. Index. Numerous black-and-white figures. xvi + 641pp. 5⅜ × 8½.
24823-2 Pa. $11.95

28 SCIENCE FICTION STORIES, H. G. Wells. Novels, *Star Begotten* and *Men Like Gods,* plus 26 short stories: "Empire of the Ants," "A Story of the Stone Age," "The Stolen Bacillus," "In the Abyss," etc. 915pp. 5⅜ × 8½. (Available in U.S. only)
20265-8 Cloth. $10.95

HANDBOOK OF PICTORIAL SYMBOLS, Rudolph Modley. 3,250 signs and symbols, many systems in full; official or heavy commercial use. Arranged by subject. Most in Pictorial Archive series. 143pp. 8¼ × 11. 23357-X Pa. $5.95

INCIDENTS OF TRAVEL IN YUCATAN, John L. Stephens. Classic (1843) exploration of jungles of Yucatan, looking for evidences of Maya civilization. Travel adventures, Mexican and Indian culture, etc. Total of 669pp. 5⅜ × 8½.
20926-1, 20927-X Pa., Two-vol. set $9.90

DEGAS: An Intimate Portrait, Ambroise Vollard. Charming, anecdotal memoir by famous art dealer of one of the greatest 19th-century French painters. 14 black-and-white illustrations. Introduction by Harold L. Van Doren. 96pp. 5⅜ × 8½.
25131-4 Pa. $3.95

PERSONAL NARRATIVE OF A PILGRIMAGE TO ALMANDINAH AND MECCAH, Richard Burton. Great travel classic by remarkably colorful personality. Burton, disguised as a Moroccan, visited sacred shrines of Islam, narrowly escaping death. 47 illustrations. 959pp. 5⅜ × 8½. 21217-3, 21218-1 Pa., Two-vol. set $19.90

PHRASE AND WORD ORIGINS, A. H. Holt. Entertaining, reliable, modern study of more than 1,200 colorful words, phrases, origins and histories. Much unexpected information. 254pp. 5⅜ × 8½. 20758-7 Pa. $4.95

THE RED THUMB MARK, R. Austin Freeman. In this first Dr. Thorndyke case, the great scientific detective draws fascinating conclusions from the nature of a single fingerprint. Exciting story, authentic science. 320pp. 5⅜ × 8½. (Available in U.S. only) 25210-8 Pa. $5.95

AN EGYPTIAN HIEROGLYPHIC DICTIONARY, E. A. Wallis Budge. Monumental work containing about 25,000 words or terms that occur in texts ranging from 3000 B.C. to 600 A.D. Each entry consists of a transliteration of the word, the word in hieroglyphs, and the meaning in English. 1,314pp. 6⅝ × 10.
23615-3, 23616-1 Pa., Two-vol. set $27.90

THE COMPLEAT STRATEGYST: Being a Primer on the Theory of Games of Strategy, J. D. Williams. Highly entertaining classic describes, with many illustrated examples, how to select best strategies in conflict situations. Prefaces. Appendices. xvi + 268pp. 5⅜ × 8½. 25101-2 Pa. $5.95

THE ROAD TO OZ, L. Frank Baum. Dorothy meets the Shaggy Man, little Button-Bright and the Rainbow's beautiful daughter in this delightful trip to the magical Land of Oz. 272pp. 5⅜ × 8. 25208-6 Pa. $4.95

POINT AND LINE TO PLANE, Wassily Kandinsky. Seminal exposition of role of point, line, other elements in non-objective painting. Essential to understanding 20th-century art. 127 illustrations. 192pp. 6½ × 9¼. 23808-3 Pa. $4.50

LADY ANNA, Anthony Trollope. Moving chronicle of Countess Lovel's bitter struggle to win for herself and daughter Anna their rightful rank and fortune—perhaps at cost of sanity itself. 384pp. 5⅜ × 8½. 24669-8 Pa. $6.95

EGYPTIAN MAGIC, E. A. Wallis Budge. Sums up all that is known about magic in Ancient Egypt: the role of magic in controlling the gods, powerful amulets that warded off evil spirits, scarabs of immortality, use of wax images, formulas and spells, the secret name, much more. 253pp. 5⅜ × 8½. 22681-6 Pa. $4.00

THE DANCE OF SIVA, Ananda Coomaraswamy. Preeminent authority unfolds the vast metaphysic of India: the revelation of her art, conception of the universe, social organization, etc. 27 reproductions of art masterpieces. 192pp. 5⅜ × 8½.
24817-8 Pa. $5.95

CHRISTMAS CUSTOMS AND TRADITIONS, Clement A. Miles. Origin, evolution, significance of religious, secular practices. Caroling, gifts, yule logs, much more. Full, scholarly yet fascinating; non-sectarian. 400pp. 5⅜ × 8½.
23354-5 Pa. $6.50

THE HUMAN FIGURE IN MOTION, Eadweard Muybridge. More than 4,500 stopped-action photos, in action series, showing undraped men, women, children jumping, lying down, throwing, sitting, wrestling, carrying, etc. 390pp. 7⅞ × 10⅝.
20204-6 Cloth. $21.95

THE MAN WHO WAS THURSDAY, Gilbert Keith Chesterton. Witty, fast-paced novel about a club of anarchists in turn-of-the-century London. Brilliant social, religious, philosophical speculations. 128pp. 5⅜ × 8½.
25121-7 Pa. $3.95

A CEZANNE SKETCHBOOK: Figures, Portraits, Landscapes and Still Lifes, Paul Cezanne. Great artist experiments with tonal effects, light, mass, other qualities in over 100 drawings. A revealing view of developing master painter, precursor of Cubism. 102 black-and-white illustrations. 144pp. 8¾ × 6⅜.
24790-2 Pa. $5.95

AN ENCYCLOPEDIA OF BATTLES: Accounts of Over 1,560 Battles from 1479 B.C. to the Present, David Eggenberger. Presents essential details of every major battle in recorded history, from the first battle of Megiddo in 1479 B.C. to Grenada in 1984. List of Battle Maps. New Appendix covering the years 1967–1984. Index. 99 illustrations. 544pp. 6½ × 9¼.
24913-1 Pa. $14.95

AN ETYMOLOGICAL DICTIONARY OF MODERN ENGLISH, Ernest Weekley. Richest, fullest work, by foremost British lexicographer. Detailed word histories. Inexhaustible. Total of 856pp. 6½ × 9¼.
21873-2, 21874-0 Pa., Two-vol. set $17.00

WEBSTER'S AMERICAN MILITARY BIOGRAPHIES, edited by Robert McHenry. Over 1,000 figures who shaped 3 centuries of American military history. Detailed biographies of Nathan Hale, Douglas MacArthur, Mary Hallaren, others. Chronologies of engagements, more. Introduction. Addenda. 1,033 entries in alphabetical order. xi + 548pp. 6½ × 9¼. (Available in U.S. only)
24758-9 Pa. $11.95

LIFE IN ANCIENT EGYPT, Adolf Erman. Detailed older account, with much not in more recent books: domestic life, religion, magic, medicine, commerce, and whatever else needed for complete picture. Many illustrations. 597pp. 5⅜ × 8½.
22632-8 Pa. $8.50

HISTORIC COSTUME IN PICTURES, Braun & Schneider. Over 1,450 costumed figures shown, covering a wide variety of peoples: kings, emperors, nobles, priests, servants, soldiers, scholars, townsfolk, peasants, merchants, courtiers, cavaliers, and more. 256pp. 8⅜ × 11¼.
23150-X Pa. $7.95

THE NOTEBOOKS OF LEONARDO DA VINCI, edited by J. P. Richter. Extracts from manuscripts reveal great genius; on painting, sculpture, anatomy, sciences, geography, etc. Both Italian and English. 186 ms. pages reproduced, plus 500 additional drawings, including studies for *Last Supper, Sforza* monument, etc. 860pp. 7⅞ × 10¾. (Available in U.S. only) 22572-0, 22573-9 Pa., Two-vol. set $25.90

THE ART NOUVEAU STYLE BOOK OF ALPHONSE MUCHA: All 72 Plates from "Documents Decoratifs" in Original Color, Alphonse Mucha. Rare copyright-free design portfolio by high priest of Art Nouveau. Jewelry, wallpaper, stained glass, furniture, figure studies, plant and animal motifs, etc. Only complete one-volume edition. 80pp. 9⅜ × 12¼. 24044-4 Pa. $8.95

ANIMALS: 1,419 COPYRIGHT-FREE ILLUSTRATIONS OF MAMMALS, BIRDS, FISH, INSECTS, ETC., edited by Jim Harter. Clear wood engravings present, in extremely lifelike poses, over 1,000 species of animals. One of the most extensive pictorial sourcebooks of its kind. Captions. Index. 284pp. 9 × 12.
23766-4 Pa. $9.95

OBELISTS FLY HIGH, C. Daly King. Masterpiece of American detective fiction, long out of print, involves murder on a 1935 transcontinental flight—"a very thrilling story"—NY Times. Unabridged and unaltered republication of the edition published by William Collins Sons & Co. Ltd., London, 1935. 288pp. 5⅜ × 8½. (Available in U.S. only) 25036-9 Pa. $4.95

VICTORIAN AND EDWARDIAN FASHION: A Photographic Survey, Alison Gernsheim. First fashion history completely illustrated by contemporary photographs. Full text plus 235 photos, 1840–1914, in which many celebrities appear. 240pp. 6½ × 9¼. 24205-6 Pa. $6.00

THE ART OF THE FRENCH ILLUSTRATED BOOK, 1700–1914, Gordon N. Ray. Over 630 superb book illustrations by Fragonard, Delacroix, Daumier, Doré, Grandville, Manet, Mucha, Steinlen, Toulouse-Lautrec and many others. Preface. Introduction. 633 halftones. Indices of artists, authors & titles, binders and provenances. Appendices. Bibliography. 608pp. 8⅜ × 11¼. 25086-5 Pa. $24.95

THE WONDERFUL WIZARD OF OZ, L. Frank Baum. Facsimile in full color of America's finest children's classic. 143 illustrations by W. W. Denslow. 267pp. 5⅜ × 8½. 20691-2 Pa. $5.95

FRONTIERS OF MODERN PHYSICS: New Perspectives on Cosmology, Relativity, Black Holes and Extraterrestrial Intelligence, Tony Rothman, et al. For the intelligent layman. Subjects include: cosmological models of the universe; black holes; the neutrino; the search for extraterrestrial intelligence. Introduction. 46 black-and-white illustrations. 192pp. 5⅜ × 8½. 24587-X Pa. $6.95

THE FRIENDLY STARS, Martha Evans Martin & Donald Howard Menzel. Classic text marshalls the stars together in an engaging, non-technical survey, presenting them as sources of beauty in night sky. 23 illustrations. Foreword. 2 star charts. Index. 147pp. 5⅜ × 8½. 21099-5 Pa. $3.50

FADS AND FALLACIES IN THE NAME OF SCIENCE, Martin Gardner. Fair, witty appraisal of cranks, quacks, and quackeries of science and pseudoscience: hollow earth, Velikovsky, orgone energy, Dianetics, flying saucers, Bridey Murphy, food and medical fads, etc. Revised, expanded In the Name of Science. "A very able and even-tempered presentation."—The New Yorker. 363pp. 5⅜ × 8.
20394-8 Pa. $6.50

ANCIENT EGYPT: ITS CULTURE AND HISTORY, J. E Manchip White. From pre-dynastics through Ptolemies: society, history, political structure, religion, daily life, literature, cultural heritage. 48 plates. 217pp. 5⅜ × 8½. 22548-8 Pa. $4.95

SIR HARRY HOTSPUR OF HUMBLETHWAITE, Anthony Trollope. Incisive, unconventional psychological study of a conflict between a wealthy baronet, his idealistic daughter, and their scapegrace cousin. The 1870 novel in its first inexpensive edition in years. 250pp. 5⅜ × 8½. 24953-0 Pa. $5.95

LASERS AND HOLOGRAPHY, Winston E. Kock. Sound introduction to burgeoning field, expanded (1981) for second edition. Wave patterns, coherence, lasers, diffraction, zone plates, properties of holograms, recent advances. 84 illustrations. 160pp. 5⅜ × 8¼. (Except in United Kingdom) 24041-X Pa. $3.50

INTRODUCTION TO ARTIFICIAL INTELLIGENCE: SECOND, ENLARGED EDITION, Philip C. Jackson, Jr. Comprehensive survey of artificial intelligence—the study of how machines (computers) can be made to act intelligently. Includes introductory and advanced material. Extensive notes updating the main text. 132 black-and-white illustrations. 512pp. 5⅜ × 8½. 24864-X Pa. $8.95

HISTORY OF INDIAN AND INDONESIAN ART, Ananda K. Coomaraswamy. Over 400 illustrations illuminate classic study of Indian art from earliest Harappa finds to early 20th century. Provides philosophical, religious and social insights. 304pp. 6⅜ × 9⅜. 25005-9 Pa. $8.95

THE GOLEM, Gustav Meyrink. Most famous supernatural novel in modern European literature, set in Ghetto of Old Prague around 1890. Compelling story of mystical experiences, strange transformations, profound terror. 13 black-and-white illustrations. 224pp. 5⅜ × 8½. (Available in U.S. only) 25025-3 Pa. $5.95

ARMADALE, Wilkie Collins. Third great mystery novel by the author of *The Woman in White* and *The Moonstone*. Original magazine version with 40 illustrations. 597pp. 5⅜ × 8½. 23429-0 Pa. $9.95

PICTORIAL ENCYCLOPEDIA OF HISTORIC ARCHITECTURAL PLANS, DETAILS AND ELEMENTS: With 1,880 Line Drawings of Arches, Domes, Doorways, Facades, Gables, Windows, etc., John Theodore Haneman. Sourcebook of inspiration for architects, designers, others. Bibliography. Captions. 141pp. 9 × 12. 24605-1 Pa. $6.95

BENCHLEY LOST AND FOUND, Robert Benchley. Finest humor from early 30's, about pet peeves, child psychologists, post office and others. Mostly unavailable elsewhere. 73 illustrations by Peter Arno and others. 183pp. 5⅜ × 8½. 22410-4 Pa. $3.95

ERTÉ GRAPHICS, Erté. Collection of striking color graphics: *Seasons, Alphabet, Numerals, Aces* and *Precious Stones*. 50 plates, including 4 on covers. 48pp. 9⅜ × 12¼. 23580-7 Pa. $6.95

THE JOURNAL OF HENRY D. THOREAU, edited by Bradford Torrey, F. H. Allen. Complete reprinting of 14 volumes, 1837–61, over two million words; the sourcebooks for *Walden*, etc. Definitive. All original sketches, plus 75 photographs. 1,804pp. 8½ × 12¼. 20312-3, 20313-1 Cloth., Two-vol. set $80.00

CASTLES: THEIR CONSTRUCTION AND HISTORY, Sidney Toy. Traces castle development from ancient roots. Nearly 200 photographs and drawings illustrate moats, keeps, baileys, many other features. Caernarvon, Dover Castles, Hadrian's Wall, Tower of London, dozens more. 256pp. 5⅜ × 8¼. 24898-4 Pa. $5.95

AMERICAN CLIPPER SHIPS: 1833–1858, Octavius T. Howe & Frederick C. Matthews. Fully-illustrated, encyclopedic review of 352 clipper ships from the period of America's greatest maritime supremacy. Introduction. 109 halftones. 5 black-and-white line illustrations. Index. Total of 928pp. 5⅜ × 8½.

25115-2, 25116-0 Pa., Two vol. set $17.90

TOWARDS A NEW ARCHITECTURE, Le Corbusier. Pioneering manifesto by great architect, near legendary founder of "International School." Technical and aesthetic theories, views on industry, economics, relation of form to function, "mass-production spirit," much more. Profusely illustrated. Unabridged translation of 13th French edition. Introduction by Frederick Etchells. 320pp. 6⅛ × 9¼. (Available in U.S. only)

25023-7 Pa. $8.95

THE BOOK OF KELLS, edited by Blanche Cirker. Inexpensive collection of 32 full-color, full-page plates from the greatest illuminated manuscript of the Middle Ages, painstakingly reproduced from rare facsimile edition. Publisher's Note. Captions. 32pp. 9⅜ × 12¼.

24345-1 Pa. $4.95

BEST SCIENCE FICTION STORIES OF H. G. WELLS, H. G. Wells. Full novel *The Invisible Man*, plus 17 short stories: "The Crystal Egg," "Aepyornis Island," "The Strange Orchid," etc. 303pp. 5⅜ × 8½. (Available in U.S. only)

21531-8 Pa. $4.95

AMERICAN SAILING SHIPS: Their Plans and History, Charles G. Davis. Photos, construction details of schooners, frigates, clippers, other sailcraft of 18th to early 20th centuries—plus entertaining discourse on design, rigging, nautical lore, much more. 137 black-and-white illustrations. 240pp. 6⅛ × 9¼.

24658-2 Pa. $5.95

ENTERTAINING MATHEMATICAL PUZZLES, Martin Gardner. Selection of author's favorite conundrums involving arithmetic, money, speed, etc., with lively commentary. Complete solutions. 112pp. 5⅜ × 8½. 25211-6 Pa. $2.95

THE WILL TO BELIEVE, HUMAN IMMORTALITY, William James. Two books bound together. Effect of irrational on logical, and arguments for human immortality. 402pp. 5⅜ × 8½. 20291-7 Pa. $7.50

THE HAUNTED MONASTERY and THE CHINESE MAZE MURDERS, Robert Van Gulik. 2 full novels by Van Gulik continue adventures of Judge Dee and his companions. An evil Taoist monastery, seemingly supernatural events; overgrown topiary maze that hides strange crimes. Set in 7th-century China. 27 illustrations. 328pp. 5⅜ × 8½. 23502-5 Pa. $5.95

CELEBRATED CASES OF JUDGE DEE (DEE GOONG AN), translated by Robert Van Gulik. Authentic 18th-century Chinese detective novel; Dee and associates solve three interlocked cases. Led to Van Gulik's own stories with same characters. Extensive introduction. 9 illustrations. 237pp. 5⅜ × 8½.

23337-5 Pa. $4.95

Prices subject to change without notice.
Available at your book dealer or write for free catalog to Dept. GI, Dover Publications, Inc., 31 East 2nd St., Mineola, N.Y. 11501. Dover publishes more than 175 books each year on science, elementary and advanced mathematics, biology, music, art, literary history, social sciences and other areas.